7/05

D1274888

THE WORLD'S HOT SPOTS

Iraq

**Other books in the
World's Hot Spots series:**

Afghanistan
North Korea
Pakistan
The Palestinians and the Disputed Territories
Saudi Arabia

THE WORLD'S H🔥T SPOTS

Iraq

Debra A. Miller, *Book Editor*

Daniel Leone, *President*
Bonnie Szumski, *Publisher*
Scott Barbour, *Managing Editor*

GREENHAVEN
PRESS ®

THOMSON
━━━━✦━━━━ ™
GALE

San Diego • Detroit • New York • San Francisco • Cleveland
New Haven, Conn. • Waterville, Maine • London • Munich

LIBRARY OF CONGRESS CATALOGING-IN-PUBLICATION DATA

Iraq / Debra A. Miller, book editor.
  p. cm. — (The world's hot spots)
Includes bibliographical references and index.
ISBN 0-7377-1814-5 (pbk. : alk. paper) — ISBN 0-7377-1813-7 (lib. : alk. paper)
  1. Iraq. I. Miller, Debra A. II. Series.
DS70.9.I72 2004
956.7044—dc21   2003040761

Printed in the United States of America

♦ CONTENTS

Saddam Hussein and other high-level Baath Party leaders, locate and destroy weapons of mass destruction, and create an interim authority to run Iraq until elections can be held for a new government.

Chapter 3: Challenges for Postwar Iraq and the World

1. Getting Iraq's Oil Flowing
by the Economist
America and Britain promised even before the war started that they did not seek control over Iraq's oil, acknowledging that it belongs to the Iraqi people. But Iraq's oil industry is in very bad shape, and fixing it raises difficult questions about the role of U.S. and other foreign oil firms in getting Iraq's oil flowing.

2. Establishing an Interim Government in Iraq
by Mark Sedra
With the war over, disagreements have arisen over how to govern Iraq until a permanent government can be established. The plan most likely to be implemented is an occupation government led by the U.S. military that will remain in power for an indefinite period of time.

3. Democracy and Ethnic Divisions in Iraq
by Efraim Karsh
Establishing democracy in Iraq will be difficult given that historically Iraq has been plagued by ethnic conflict and has needed a strong, autocratic leader to stay united. The United States must work to create a representative style of government in which each of Iraq's major ethnic and religious groups has a voice.

4. The War in Iraq and the Demise of International Institutions
by Paul Johnson
The U.S./British war in Iraq is likely to be viewed as the first significant event of the twenty-first century. The two allies' willingness to act without the help of the United Nations and the North Atlantic Treaty Organization, and with the opprobrium of many European na-

tions, has contributed to the growing ineffectiveness of those international institutions.

5. A Destabilized Postwar World

The consequences of the war in Iraq may threaten U.S. national security. Four possible consequences include greater instability in the Middle East, an increase in terrorism, a weakening of U.S. alliances, and a rise in nuclear proliferation.

The American Heritage Dictionary defines the term *hot spot* as "an area in which there is dangerous unrest or hostile action." Though it is probably true that almost any conceivable "area" contains potentially "dangerous unrest or hostile action," there are certain countries in the world especially susceptible to conflict that threatens the lives of noncombatants on a regular basis. After the events of September 11, 2001, the consequences of this particular kind of conflict and the importance of the countries, regions, or groups that produce it are even more relevant for all concerned public policy makers, citizens, and students. Perhaps now more than ever, the violence and instability that engulfs the world's hot spots truly has a global reach and demands the attention of the entire international community.

The scope of problems caused by regional conflicts is evident in the extent to which international policy makers have begun to assert themselves in efforts to reduce the tension and violence that threatens innocent lives around the globe. The U.S. Congress, for example, recently addressed the issue of economic stability in Pakistan by considering a trading bill to encourage growth in the Pakistani textile industry. The efforts of some congresspeople to improve the economic conditions in Pakistan through trade with the United States was more than an effort to address a potential economic cause of the instability engulfing Pakistani society. It was also an acknowledgment that domestic issues in Pakistan are connected to domestic political issues in the United States. Without a concerted effort by policy makers in the United States, or any other country for that matter, it is quite possible that the violence and instability that shatters the lives of Pakistanis will not only continue, but will also worsen and threaten the stability and prosperity of other regions.

Recent international efforts to reach a peaceful settlement of the Israeli-Palestinian conflict also demonstrate how peace and stability in the Middle East is not just a regional issue. The toll on Palestinian and Israeli lives is easy to see through the suicide bombings and rocket attacks in Israeli cities and in the occupied territories of the West Bank and Gaza. What is, perhaps, not as evident is the extent to which this conflict involves the rest of the world. Saudi Arabia and Iran, for instance, have long been at odds and have attempted to gain control of the conflict by supporting competing organizations dedicated to a Palestinian state. These groups have often used Saudi and Iranian financial and political support to carry out violent attacks against Israeli civilians and military installations. Of course, the issue goes far beyond a struggle between two regional powers to gain control of the region's most visible issue. Many analysts and leaders have also argued that the West's military and political support of Israel is one of the leading factors that motivated al-Qaeda's September 11 attacks on New York and Washington, D.C. In many ways, this regional conflict is an international affair that will require international solutions.

The World's Hot Spots series is intended to meet the demand for information and discussion among young adults and students who would like to better understand the areas embroiled in conflicts that contribute to catastrophic events like those of September 11. Each volume of The World's Hot Spots is an anthology of primary and secondary documents that provides historical background to the conflict, or conflicts, under examination. The books also provide students with a wide range of opinions from world leaders, activists, and professional writers concerning the root causes and potential solutions to the problems facing the countries covered in this series. In addition, extensive research tools such as an annotated table of contents, bibliography, and glossaries of terms and important figures provide readers a foundation from which they can build their knowledge of some of the world's most pressing issues. The information and opinions presented in The World's Hot Spots series will give students some of the tools they will need to become active participants in the ongoing dialogue concerning the globe's most volatile regions.

♦ INTRODUCTION

I n the dark of night on March 19, 2003, U.S. B-2 Spirit bombers and F-117 Nighthawk stealth fighter jets flew toward a target in Baghdad, the capital city of Iraq, on a surprise mission to kill Saddam Hussein and his top aides and topple his regime. The United States hoped, in one decisive blow, to accomplish its goal of ending Hussein's twenty-four-year-old dictatorship in Iraq and derail his plans to develop weapons of mass destruction. Although the surgical strike on Hussein would later be shown to be a failure, the United States also had begun to set the stage for a planned all-out air and land assault on Iraq. On March 21, 2003, the long-awaited military campaign against Iraq began. Designed by the Pentagon to produce "shock and awe" in Iraqi troops, the first round of air strikes involved the dropping of more than thirteen hundred cruise missiles and bombs on command and control targets in Baghdad as ground forces began a march toward the city. The war continued for a mere three weeks; President George W. Bush declared on April 15, 2003, that "the regime of Saddam Hussein is no more."[1]

The attack on Iraq was launched by the United States and Great Britain and a coalition of twenty-eight other countries, mostly eastern European and smaller nations, dubbed by U.S. officials as a "coalition of the willing." However, the war was largely a unilateral, U.S.-initiated action without specific consent from the United Nations (UN). It followed a protracted thirteen-month period of debate and diplomacy in which the United States attempted but failed to attain international support for forcing a regime change in Iraq.

The March Toward War

Iraq became the focus of U.S. military interest after the September 11, 2001, terrorist attacks on America, which precipitated a general U.S. war against terrorism. The first warning to Iraq came in President Bush's State of the Union address to the nation on January 29, 2002, when he announced that Iraq, Iran, and North Korea were part of an "axis of evil" that threatened the peace of the world. Bush explained that Iraq supported terror, flaunted its hostility toward America, and had been trying to develop biological, chemical, and nuclear weapons for over a decade. By seeking weapons of mass destruction (WMD), the president claimed, Iraq posed a grave danger because it could provide arms to terrorists, attack America's allies, or blackmail the United States. America, the president warned, "will not permit the world's most dangerous regimes to threaten us with the world's most destructive weapons."[2]

Throughout 2002 people in the United States and around the world debated whether America should attack Iraq to depose Hussein. The president's supporters argued that it was important to remove Hussein from power before he was able to fully develop his WMD capabilities. In a speech on August 26, 2002, for example, Vice President Dick Cheney warned,

> Armed with an arsenal of these weapons of terror, and seated atop ten percent of the world's oil reserves, Saddam Hussein could then be expected to seek domination of the entire Middle East, take control of a great portion of the world's energy supplies, directly threaten America's friends throughout the region, and subject the United States or any other nation to nuclear blackmail.[3]

The president, however, was harshly criticized for proposing a unilateral military action against another country that did not constitute an imminent threat to the United States. His detractors pointed out that there was no clear evidence that Hussein possessed nuclear or missile capabilities that would pose a current threat, nor was there a proven link between Iraq and terrorism. In addition, critics argued that America's European allies strongly opposed a military strike, that Arabs in the region would be outraged by a U.S. invasion of an Arab country such as Iraq, and that there was no plan to stabilize Iraq after Hussein was removed from power. Further, the cost of a unilateral war, critics said, would be astronomical for the United States. Some also suggested that the push for regime change in Iraq had little to do with a WMD threat and had much more to do with the desire to establish a friendly government in Iraq in order to ensure America's continued access to important Iraqi oil reserves; Iraq's reserves are the second largest in the world and constitute a significant portion of U.S. oil imports.

A consensus eventually developed for diplomatic efforts as an alternative to military action. Supporters of this approach sought to reinvigorate weapons inspections that were started in the early 1990s by the UN but were suspended in 1998. After European allies such as France and Britain urged the United States to avoid unilateral action and work with the UN contain the Iraqi threat, President Bush appeared to listen. On September 12, 2002, in an address to the United Nations, Bush set forth the case against Hussein, citing the numerous UN resolutions concerning Iraq that had been ignored by the Iraqi leader. Bush also pointed out that Hussein had enjoyed a four-year period in which to rebuild his weapons arsenals since UN inspectors were last allowed into Iraq. Calling Hussein's regime "a grave and growing danger," Bush insisted that Iraq must disarm, and he urged the United Nations to develop a resolution to return weapons inspectors to Iraq. Bush's UN speech was praised by European and some Arab countries, as well as by analysts at home, and U.S. diplomats began working with other nations to develop the appropriate UN resolutions.

On November 8, 2002, the United States and Britain succeeded in getting Resolution 1441 adopted by a unanimous vote of the UN Security Council. The resolution provided Iraq a final opportunity to comply with UN disarmament obligations and set up a new program of weapons inspections with the goal of finally forcing Hussein to disarm. The resolution gave Iraq thirty days to provide the UN with a declaration detailing its programs to develop chemical, biological, and nuclear weapons as well as ballistic missiles. Also, in what the United States and others interpreted as a thinly disguised threat of military action, the resolution warned Iraq that it would "face serious consequences"[4] if it failed to comply. Iraq agreed to admit weapons inspectors. Inspections by the International Atomic Energy Agency (IAEA) and the newly formed UN weapons inspection team, called the UN Monitoring, Verification, and Inspection Commission (UNMOVIC), began in late November 2002.

However, Iraq was less than fully cooperative with the inspections process. For example, although UNMOVIC and the IAEA reported to the UN that they received access to Iraqi facilities, Iraq's declaration of weapons required by the resolution failed to account for weapons known to have existed. In addition, Iraq refused to allow Iraqi scientists to submit to private interviews with UN inspectors and raised objections to spy planes flying over Iraq to look for evidence that weapons were being hidden from inspectors. Ultimately, although no weapons of mass destruction were discovered by inspectors, the United States and Britain concluded that Iraq was continuing its deception and had failed to disarm. On February 24, 2003, the United States, Britain, and Spain circulated a second UN resolution to authorize war against Iraq.

U.S. diplomacy failed to obtain UN support at this crucial hour. Several other members of the UN Security Council, particularly France, Germany, Russia, and China, urged that inspections be given more time and openly opposed military action against Iraq. As weeks passed, it became increasingly clear that the United States could not muster the nine Security Council votes it needed to pass the second resolution; further, even if the United States did get enough votes, a veto by France or Russia seemed probable. The United States and Britain thus decided to go it alone in pursuing war against Iraq, without the blessing of the UN and without traditional western European allies; the two nations claimed they had authority to act under the "serious consequences" language of Resolution 1441.

The opposition the United States faced at the UN in large part reflected the antiwar sentiments of people around the world. Not only in Europe but also in Asia, South America, and the Middle East, hundreds of peace rallies were held denouncing the U.S. rush to war. Indeed, even in the United States antiwar protests drew crowds that numbered, in some cases, in the hundreds of thousands.

Ancient Iraq to Saddam Hussein

This crisis in Iraq, of course, did not develop overnight. Saddam Hussein had been in power since 1979, and during the 1980s he was actually the beneficiary of massive military aid from the United States and Europe; this aid, some argue, helped him to develop his weapons programs in the first place. In fact, Hussein, essentially a tribal leader skilled at strong-arm tactics against Iraqi political foes but less ex-

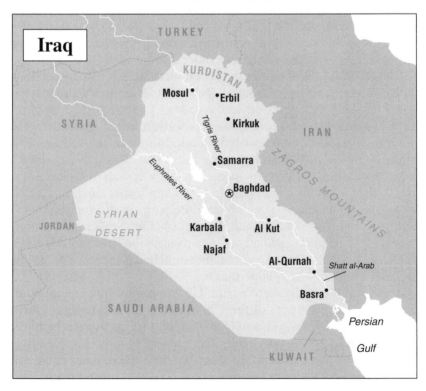

perienced with foreign policy, became an enemy of the United States only after a series of events increased his wealth and power and caused him to be seen as a threat to other countries. For example, rising prices of oil in the 1970s provided Iraq with newfound economic power, a war with Iran in the 1980s (and support from the United States and other nations) increased his military capabilities, and in 1990 he became aggressive toward Kuwait.

Indeed, Hussein's aggression and the turmoil it caused is only one chapter of a long history of political instability and repression in Iraq. Although Iraq has a very long history, it only recently emerged as an independent nation. Before then, Muslims ruled a thriving Arab empire in the Middle East. This unity weakened when a schism developed between two Muslim sects, the Sunnis and the Shias (also called Shiites). The area now known as Iraq was then conquered by the followers of Genghis Khan during the thirteenth century and by the Turks during the sixteenth century. Thereafter, Iraq remained part of the Ottoman Empire for a period of nearly four hundred years.

During the twentieth century the outbreak of World War I and Turkey's entrance into the war on the side of the Germans caused the British to invade Turk-controlled areas such as Basra and Baghdad. Hopes for Arab independence after the collapse of Ottoman rule were dashed in 1920, when Britain quashed a united Sunni-Shia revolt against postwar British rule. Britain installed a colonial monarchy headed by a Syrian, King Faisal, and the boundaries for the modern state of Iraq were drawn. Unfortunately, the new state included an area near Turkey that was inhabited by a non-Arab ethnic group called the Kurds, whose culture and history is distinct from both the Sunnis and the Shias, creating yet a third ethnic faction in the newly formed state. Iraq became a sovereign state in 1932, but it continued to suffer from political unrest and disunity.

In 1958 the monarchy was overthrown in a coup led by military officer Abdul Karim Kassem. Kassem himself was overthrown just a few years later, in 1963, by the Baath Party, a political sect that developed in opposition to the monarchy. The party, however, initially lacked a coherent program to run the country and was quickly overtaken in another coup by military officers. However, led by a group of Sunni Arabs from the town of Tikrīt, who were united by tribal and family ties, the party was able to reacquire power in 1968.

Saddam Hussein was part of this Sunni tribe from Tikrīt and rose to power as part of the new Baath Party. He was a cousin to Ahmad Hasan al Bakr, a respected military leader who became president of the Baath Party's new government in Iraq. For many years Hussein operated behind the scenes as Bakr's ruthless commander of the Baath

Party's security system, helping the party to establish a repressive dictatorship. Finally, Hussein seized the presidency of Iraq from Bakr in 1979 and immediately carried out a reign of terror designed to eliminate all opposition and establish his complete control of Iraq.

At the time of Hussein's rise to power, Iraq was experiencing a growth in wealth, thanks to its oil resources and increases in oil prices during the 1970s. Hussein used this wealth to implement economic development programs that allowed many Iraqis to rise to middle-class status, to strengthen his armies, and to consolidate his totalitarian grip on power. Using these economic incentives and repression, Hussein succeeded in uniting Iraq's three disparate ethnic groups (Sunnis, Shias, and Kurds) more successfully than at any other time in Iraq's history. Hussein next turned his attention to increasing Iraq's power among Arab nations in the Middle East. His first exercise of that power came in 1980, when Iraq invaded Iran.

The Iran-Iraq War and the Growth of Iraqi Military Might

In 1979 the Islamic revolution in Iran, led by the Ayatollah Khomeini, threatened to awaken the dissatisfaction of Iraq's Shia Muslims. For much of Iraqi history, the Shias, although a majority of the population, had been excluded from the exercise of political or economic power in Iraq, which was ruled by Sunnis. Iran encouraged Shia demonstrations in Iraq, and ultimately Iraq attacked Iran in 1980, leading to a protracted seven-year war.

Initially, the Iraqi army seemed no match for the Iranians, but fears of the revolutionary, fundamentalist Islamic government in Iran caused many countries to come to Iraq's aid. Neighboring Arab nations lent their support, and the Soviet Union and European nations such as France and Britain provided arms to Iraq. Indeed, France provided Iraq with a nuclear reactor, which was later destroyed by Israel in a unilateral strike during the early 1980s. After Iran began attacking ships carrying oil in the Persian Gulf, the United States protected the flow of oil by allowing Kuwaiti oil tankers to be registered as American ships; thus registered, the ships would be less vulnerable to attack because Iran would not want to anger the United States and wind up fighting that powerful country. Thereafter, the United States became involved on the Iraqi side and provided billions of dollars of military aid to Iraq.

The Iran-Iraq War ended through a UN-sponsored cease-fire in 1987. The war produced no victory for either side but cost as many as 367,000 lives and resulted in massive economic disruption for both countries. Iraq emerged from the war crippled economically but with a strong military. Also, Iraq now had chemical weapons, which Hussein had used during the 1980s both against Iran and internally against Kurdish civilians.

The Kuwait Invasion and Its Aftermath

After the war with Iran, Hussein sought to rebuild Iraq economically. In 1990 he became concerned that overproduction of oil was depressing oil prices. Specifically, Hussein accused Kuwait of flooding the market in violation of the production quotas set by the Organization of Petroleum Exporting Countries, causing a drop in Iraq's oil revenues at a time when Hussein most needed funds. Hussein saw a conspiracy between Kuwait and other countries (including the United States) to lower oil prices. He demanded that Kuwait pay Iraq $2.4 billion in oil revenues from disputed oil fields in Rumaila, on the border between the two countries. He also insisted that Kuwait write off debts that Iraq owed it since the Iran-Iraq War.

Other Arab countries, also incensed at Kuwait's actions, sought to mediate the dispute to no avail. When Kuwait showed no interest in giving in to Iraq's demands, Iraq invaded Kuwait on August 2, 1990, and quickly took control of the country. The invasion may have been one of Hussein's biggest miscalculations, however, because the UN Security Council immediately responded with a unanimous resolution condemning the invasion and demanding Iraq's withdrawal. Most Arab nations also called for Iraqi withdrawal.

The Iraqi invasion of Kuwait, and Hussein's refusal to withdraw, set in motion a series of events that have had profound consequences for Iraq. The United States was able to develop a coalition that included not only traditional European allies and members of the UN Security Council but also Turkey, Saudi Arabia, and other Arab countries. The UN voted to impose economic sanctions against Iraq in an attempt to force Hussein to withdraw and disarm. When Hussein did not leave Kuwait, a massive military attack called Operation Desert Storm was authorized by the United Nations and launched by the United States and its allies on January 16, 1991.

The Gulf War lasted only a few short months, but the effects of the war and the accompanying sanctions on the Iraqi people are still being felt today. The military attack accomplished its stated goals of destroying much of Iraq's military arsenal (including nuclear and chemical facilities) and liberating Kuwait. The war, however, also destroyed much of the country's urban infrastructure, including irrigation, water, and sewage systems, which resulted in a lack of clean water, disease, and food shortages.

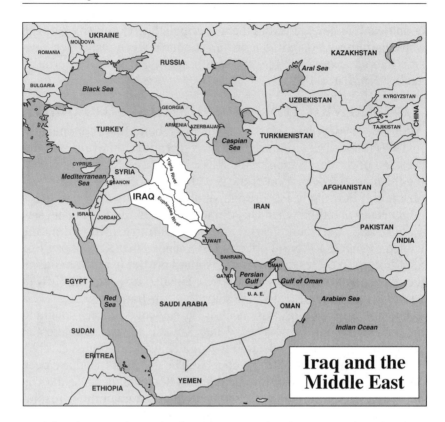

Iraq and the Middle East

After the war the United Nations voted to keep sanctions in place until all of Iraq's WMD programs were destroyed. A weapons inspection team, called the United Nations Special Commission on Iraq (UNSCOM), was assembled to supervise the disarming, and in the years that followed, UNSCOM uncovered and destroyed much of Iraq's WMD arsenal. Hussein, however, made the inspections difficult by blocking access to weapons sites, lying about the extent or existence of weapons programs, and generally defying the process whenever possible. Slowly, Hussein managed to weaken the weapons inspections and limit inspectors' activities. For example, in 1997 he declared several sites to be "presidential" and negotiated with the United Nations to respect Iraq's sovereignty at those sites. Later, Hussein further restricted inspections and accused the United States of using UNSCOM as a vehicle for spying on Iraq, leading to a suspension of weapons inspections in 1998.

The economic sanctions on Iraq, however, continued. Many have criticized the sanctions on humanitarian grounds, arguing that they have caused unjustified suffering for the Iraqi people without hurting Saddam Hussein. Clearly, sanctions devastated the Iraqi economy, impoverished the middle class, and created severe health and food crises. Some have estimated that as many as five hundred thousand Iraqi children have died as a result of the sanctions. The United Nations tried to respond to these humanitarian problems by authorizing an oil-for-food program in which Iraq was allowed to sell oil to purchase food, medicine, and other necessities. The program helped ease the effect of the sanctions, but in many cases Hussein refused to purchase humanitarian items for his people, preferring instead to sell oil on the black market to acquire money to bolster support for his regime. The sanctions, however, did limit to some degree Hussein's ability to import items that could be used to produce conventional as well as nuclear and biological weapons.

More than ten years after Hussein invaded Kuwait, his country lay in ruins, his people were starving, his economy was shattered, and his military was significantly weakened. Yet he had managed to halt weapons inspections and weaken sanctions. He had watched the broad coalition of nations that attacked him in 1991 fall apart. No opposition groups had overthrown him. His regime had survived, and many feared that he was once again developing weapons of mass destruction, including nuclear weapons and the missiles to launch them. It was this fear that, especially after the September 11, 2001, terrorist attacks, caused the United States to begin its campaign to return to Iraq to depose Saddam Hussein.

The New Iraq

Analysts now say, however, that the 2003 overthrow of Hussein's regime was the easy part. The hard part is the job of nation building that is necessary to forge a new, democratic Iraq from what is now a country shattered by three decades of repression and terror, twelve years of economic sanctions, and two U.S. wars. Tasks include everything from restoring order, feeding the population, and turning on the electricity to rebuilding the economy and oil industry, repairing infrastructure, and creating a new democratic government. Challenges are daunting: The coalition, for example, must prevent ethnic hostilities in Iraq from exploding and address Arab suspicions about a U.S. occupation of Arab lands. The war also raises many questions about the value of the UN and traditional international alliances of the past, the use or misuse of American power in the twenty-first century, and the long-term effects of the war on Arab terrorism and WMD proliferation around the globe. Whether the U.S. war in Iraq will be recorded by history as a success or a failure will likely depend on how America responds to postwar challenges and how the rest of the world judges American motives and actions.

Notes

1. Quoted in David E. Sanger and Thom Shanker, "Bush Says Regime in Iraq Is No More; Syria Is Penalized," *New York Times*, April 15, 2003.
2. George W. Bush, State of the Union Address, Washington, D.C., January 29, 2002.
3. Dick Cheney, speech at the Veterans of Foreign Wars 103rd National Convention, August 26, 2002.
4. Resolution 1441, adopted by the United Nations at Security Council meeting 4644, November 8, 2002. Available at Cable News Network, www.cnn.com.

CHAPTER 1

Historical Context

Iraq's History of Political Conflict

By Mark Lewis

The following excerpt from a Library of Congress publication describes Iraq as a country with a history of political instability characterized by coups, conspiracies, and repression in which political power is exercised only by an elite few, leaving the majority of Iraqis divorced from the political process. The excerpt traces Iraq's journey from a disorganized collection of ethnically diverse tribes that fought over the food-producing land in the valleys of the Tigris and Euphrates Rivers to the time of the Ottoman rule, when legal reforms created private property and a division between wealthy tribal leaders and impoverished tribesmen. Finally, in 1920 Iraq was subjected to British colonial rule, which created the nation's boundaries without regard to ethnic affiliations, alienated ordinary Iraqis from the political process, and resolved conflicts through repression rather than through the creation of power-sharing institutions. The present dictatorship, led by Saddam Hussein, along with rising oil revenues, provided Iraqis a brief period of stability, but this did not last long.

Iraq, a republic since the 1958 coup d' état that ended the reign of King Faisal II, became a sovereign, independent state in 1932. Although the modern state, the Republic of Iraq, is quite young, the history of the land and its people dates back more than 5,000 years. Indeed, Iraq contains the world's richest known archaeological sites. Here, in ancient Mesopotamia (the land between the rivers), the first civilization—that of Sumer—appeared in the Middle East. Despite the millennium separating the two epochs, Iraqi history displays a continuity shaped by adaptation to the ebbings and flowings of the Tigris and Euphrates rivers (in Arabic, the Dijlis and Furat, respectively). Allowed to flow unchecked, the rivers wrought destruction in terrible floods that inundated whole towns. When the rivers were

Mark Lewis, "Historical Setting," *Iraq: A Country Study*, edited by Helen Chapin Metz. Washington, DC: Library of Congress, 1990.

controlled by irrigation dikes and other waterworks, the land became extremely fertile.

Geography and Political Fragmentation

The dual nature of the Tigris and the Euphrates—their potential to be destructive or productive—has resulted in two distinct legacies found throughout Iraqi history. On the one hand, Mesopotamia's plentiful water resources and lush river valleys allowed for the production of surplus food that served as the basis for the civilizing trend begun at Sumer and preserved by rulers such as Hammurabi (1792–1750 B.C.), Cyrus (550–530 B.C.), Darius (520–485 B.C.), Alexander (336–323 B.C.), and the Abbasids (A.D. 750–1258). The ancient cities of Sumer, Babylon, and Assyria all were located in what is now Iraq. Surplus food production and joint irrigation and flood control efforts facilitated the growth of a powerful and expanding state.

Mesopotamia could also be an extremely threatening environment, however, driving its peoples to seek security from the vicissitudes of nature. Throughout Iraqi history, various groups have formed autonomous, self-contained social units. Allegiance to ancient religious deities at Ur and Eridu, membership in the Shiat Ali (or party of Ali, the small group of followers that supported Ali ibn Abu Talib as rightful leader of the Islamic community in the seventh century), residence in the *asnaf* (guilds) or the *mahallat* (city quarters) of Baghdad under the Ottoman Turks, membership in one of a multitude of tribes—such efforts to build autonomous security-providing structures have exerted a powerful centrifugal force on Iraqi culture.

Two other factors that have inhibited political centralization are the absence of stone and Iraq's geographic location as the eastern flank of the Arab world. For much of Iraqi history, the lack of stone has severely hindered the building of roads. As a result, many parts of the country have remained beyond government control. Also, because it borders non-Arab Turkey and Iran and because of the great agricultural potential of its river valley, Iraq has attracted waves of ethnically diverse migrations. Although this influx of people has enriched Iraqi culture, it also has disrupted the country's internal balance and has led to deep-seated schisms.

Tribal Conflicts

Throughout Iraqi history, the conflict between political fragmentation and centralization has been reflected in the struggles among tribes and cities for the food-producing flatlands of the river valleys. When a central power neglected to keep the waterworks in repair, land fell into disuse, and tribes attacked settled peoples for precious and scarce agricultural commodities. For nearly 600 years, between the collapse of the Abbasid Empire in the thirteenth century and the waning years of the Ottoman era in the late nineteenth century, government authority was tenuous and tribal Iraq was, in effect, autonomous. At the beginning of the twentieth century, Iraq's disconnected, and often antagonistic, ethnic, religious, and tribal social groups professed little or no allegiance to the central government. As a result, the all-consuming concern of contemporary Iraqi history has been the forging of a nation-state out of this diverse and conflict-ridden social structure and the concomitant transformation of parochial loyalties, both tribal and ethnic, into a national identity.

Beginning in the middle of the nineteenth century, the *tanzimat* reforms (an administrative and legal reorganization of the Ottoman Empire), the emergence of private property, and the tying of Iraq to the world capitalist market severely altered Iraq's social structure. Tribal shaykhs [leaders or chiefs] traditionally had provided both spiritual leadership and tribal security. Land reform and increasing links with the West transformed many shaykhs into profit-seeking landlords, whose tribesmen became impoverished sharecroppers. Moreover, as Western economic penetration increased, the products of Iraq's once-prosperous craftsmen were displaced by machine-made British textiles.

The British Monarchy

During the twentieth century, as the power of tribal Iraq waned, Baghdad benefited from the rise of a centralized governmental apparatus, a burgeoning bureaucracy, increased educational opportunities, and the growth of the oil industry. The transformation of the urban-tribal balance resulted in a massive rural-to-urban migration. The disruption of existing parochial loyalties and the rise of new class relations based on economics fueled frequent tribal rebellions and urban uprisings during much of the twentieth century.

Iraq's social fabric was in the throes of a destabilizing transition in the first half of the twentieth century. At the same time, because of its foreign roots, the Iraqi political system suffered from a severe legitimacy crisis. Beginning with its League of Nations mandate in 1920, the British government had laid out the institutional framework for Iraqi government and politics. Britain imposed a Hashimite (also seen as Hashemite) monarchy, defined the territorial limits of Iraq with little correspondence to natural frontiers or traditional tribal and ethnic settlements, and influenced the writing of a constitution and the structure of parliament. The British also supported narrowly based groups—such as the tribal shaykhs—over the growing, urban-based nationalist movement, and resorted to military force when British interests were threatened, as in the 1941 Rashid Ali coup.

Between 1918 and 1958, British policy in Iraq had far-reaching effects. The majority of Iraqis were divorced from the political process, and the process itself failed to develop procedures for resolving internal conflicts other than rule by decree and the frequent use of repressive measures. Also, because the formative experiences of Iraq's post-1958 political leadership centered around clandestine opposition activity, decision making and government activity in general have been veiled in secrecy. Furthermore, because the country lacks deeply rooted national political institutions, political power frequently has been monopolized by a small elite, the members of which are often bound by close family or tribal ties.

After the Monarchy

Between the overthrow of the monarchy in 1958 and the emergence of Saddam Husayn in the mid-1970s, Iraqi history was a chronicle of conspiracies, coups, countercoups, and fierce Kurdish uprisings. Beginning in 1975, however, with the signing of the Algiers Agreement—an agreement between Saddam Husayn and the shah of Iran that effectively ended Iranian military support for the Kurds in Iraq—Saddam Husayn was able to bring Iraq an unprecedented period of stability. He effectively used rising oil revenues to fund large-scale development projects, to increase public sector employment, and significantly to improve education and health care. This tied increasing numbers of Iraqis to the ruling Baath (Arab Socialist Resurrection) Party. As a result, for the first time in contemporary Iraqi history, an Iraqi leader successfully forged a national identity out of Iraq's diverse social structure. Saddam Husayn's achievements and Iraq's general prosperity, however, did not survive long.

The Rise of Saddam Hussein

By Andrew Cockburn and Patrick Cockburn

*The following excerpt was written by two experienced Middle East com-
mentators, Patrick Cockburn and Andrew Cockburn. Patrick Cockburn has
been a senior Middle East correspondent for the* Financial Times *and the*
London Independent *since 1979. Andrew Cockburn is the author of several
books on defense and international affairs and coproduced a 1991 PBS doc-
umentary on Iraq. The Cockburns describe how Saddam Hussein rose to
power as part of the Baath Party, a political group dominated by Sunni Arabs
with tribal and family ties. When Hussein became president of Iraq in 1979,
he immediately purged the party of all opposition, giving him total control at
a time when Iraq was increasing its wealth as a result of rising oil prices.
Hussein was able to use this wealth to stabilize his regime; thereafter, he
turned his attention to increasing his power on the world stage.*

An Iraqi proverb says: "Two Iraqis, three sects." In Iraq, Islam
does not unify, it divides. The Sunni Arabs living in the triangle
of territory between Baghdad, Mosul, and the Syrian border are a
fifth of the population but have always dominated Iraqi governments.
The Shia Muslims make up over half the population and are the overwhelming majority in southern Iraq between Baghdad and Basra. In
the capital, they outnumber the Sunni, though governments have tried
to limit their immigration. In the north, the Kurds are a further fifth
of the Iraqi population, living in the mountains along the Iranian and
Turkish borders and the plains immediately below. . . .

Political Instability After the Monarchy

The fall of the monarchy [in 1958] ushered in a ten-year period of
military coups, countercoups, and conspiracies. The price of failure

increased by the year. [Abd al-Karim] Qassim [the army officer who overthrew the monarchy] was overthrown and killed in a bloodbath in 1963 in which five thousand were slaughtered, many of them after being tortured. It was the height of the cold war. The United States became increasingly involved after the overthrow of the British-backed monarchy. In 1959, Allen Dulles, the director of the CIA, told the Senate Foreign Relations Committee: "Iraq today is the most dangerous spot on earth." The monarchy was weak, but its successors were even weaker. The Arab nationalism of the new leaders seemed like a mask for Sunni Arab domination to the Iraqi Shia and had no appeal for the Kurds. Kurdish nationalism was growing in strength and its leaders were soon in a semipermanent state of rebellion.

Saddam Hussein's Sunni Arab Tribal Roots

Saddam Hussein al-Tikriti, who was to determine the fate of Iraq for most of the second half of the century, came of age at a critical moment in the history of Iraq. He was twenty-one when the monarchy was overthrown. Over the next decade, he learned the bloody mechanics of Iraqi politics. By 1968, he showed that he understood them perfectly. When he was only thirty-one years old, he helped engineer the two coups, within two weeks of each other, in which the Arab nationalist Baath Party, led largely by men from his home district of Tikrit, seized power. The political musical chairs of the previous ten years ended. Saddam and his party are still in power thirty years later. In later years, Saddam liked to portray himself as a man who succeeded in the face of adversity. By the 1980s, Iraqi poets were winning prizes for drawing parallels between Saddam and the Prophet Mohammed, both of whom were orphaned at an early age. In reality, Saddam came from a Sunni Arab family with just the right connections to propel him to the front of Iraqi politics. . . .

The strength of Saddam's family and clan connections matter because he was born into a tribal society. He has maintained many of its characteristics throughout his life. It was a world of intense loyalties within the clan, but cruel and hostile to outsiders. "Myself and my cousin against the world," says an old Arab proverb. Saddam later painted a picture of a deprived childhood, claiming his stepfather would rouse him at dawn by saying: "Get up, you son of a whore, go tend the sheep." His critics also stressed early traumas to prove that he came from a dysfunctional family. In fact, his reliance on his half-brothers—Barzan, Sabawi, and Watban—and his cousins, like Ali Hassan al-Majid, to stock the senior ranks of his regime argue that his inner family was always tightly knit against the outside world, whatever its inner tensions.

Hussein's Military Connections

Saddam came from the al-Bejat clan, part of the Albu Nasir tribe, which was strong in and around the nondescript town of Tikrit, on the Tigris a hundred miles north of the capital. Set on low bluffs above the river, Tikrit was a decayed textile town, once known for building rafts to carry melons to Baghdad. In so far as it was famous for anything, it was as the birthplace in the early twelfth century of Saladin, the Arab hero, though of Kurdish background, who defeated the Crusaders. Otherwise, Tikrit made little mark on Iraqi history. Its inhabitants were Arab Sunni with a curious reputation for being long-winded. "To talk like a Tikriti" is an Iraqi saying meaning to be too garrulous. By the time Saddam was growing up, the town no longer depended on trade and agriculture alone. Its young men increasingly took the road to Baghdad to get jobs in the government and, above all, in the army. . . . It was young men, often the sons of petty trades-men and landowners, from provincial towns like Tikrit on the upper Tigris and Euphrates, who saw the army as a route to power.

"One of my uncles was a nationalist, an officer in the Iraqi army," Saddam later recalled in a rare interview about his background. . . . Other relatives also reached important positions in the army. One of them, Ahmed Hassan al-Bakr, a reserved, quiet-spoken, but very am-bitious brigadier, had a critical influence on Saddam's career. He was one of the rebel officers who took part in the overthrow of the monarchy in 1958 and later quarreled with Qassim. He was born in 1914 into a family of petty notables who traditionally produced lead-ers for the Bejat clan. He was a leader of the 1963 coup, after which he became prime minister. Given that Iraqi politics at this time were dominated by the military elite, Saddam, who never entered the army, could only have risen to power in tandem with a senior mili-tary officer. . . .

Hussein's Violent Youth

The Iraqi countryside was a violent place in which everybody car-ried firearms. At first the family wanted Saddam to be a farmer, but at the age of eight, Adnan, his cousin, the son of Khairallah Tulfah and later Iraq's defense minister, told Saddam that he was learning to read and write in Tikrit. Saddam was unable to persuade his fam-ily to let him go to school. One day before dawn he set off across the fields to make his own way there. On the road he met some relatives, who approved of his educational plans and agreed to help him. Their response underlines the degree of insecurity in provincial Iraq in the 1950s. "They gave him a pistol and sent him off in a car to Tikrit," says his official biographer. Accounts of Saddam's early blood-thirstiness are suspect, but Dr. Abdul Wahad al-Hakim, an Iraqi exile, says Saddam was quite prepared to use his fearsome reputation in the next few years. He recalls:

"My headmaster told me that he wanted to expel Saddam from school. When Saddam heard about this decision, he came to his headmaster's room and threatened him with death. He said: 'I will kill you if you do not withdraw your threat against me to expel me from the school.'" At the age of ten, Saddam went to stay with Khairallah Tulfah in Baghdad, but with frequent trips home to Ouija and Tikrit.

Later, after Saddam's ascent to power, "Tikritis" was to become a nickname for the Iraqi political elite. But after the overthrow of the king in 1958, Tikrit was intensely and violently divided between Communists and nationalists such as Saddam. This is the background to the first killing by Saddam for which there is reliable evidence. The victim was Haji Sadoun al-Tikriti, a warrant officer and Communist leader in the city. It happened in 1959, and the dead man was said to be a distant relative of Saddam's. Twenty years later, Saddam, by now vice chairman of the Revolution Command Council, came to the school of a relative of the dead man in Baghdad. Following tribal tradition, he gave him blood money and a Browning pistol.

Hussein's Early Years in the Baath Party

Saddam joined the Baath Party when he was twenty, the year before the overthrow of the monarchy. Founded in Iraq in 1952, it was small and tightly organized in cells of three to seven members. Its ideology combined intense Arab nationalism with woolly socialism. Its will to power always exceeded its idea of what to do with it. Hanna Batatu, the great Iraqi historian of these years, writes: "A Baathi would have looked in vain through the whole literature of his party for a single objective analysis of any of the serious problems besetting Iraq."

But there was nothing vague about how the Baath Party intended to deal with its enemies. It had quarreled with Qassim immediately after he took power because of his opposition to pan-Arab unity with Egypt and Syria. In their first independent initiative, the Baathists decided to assassinate him. Among those recruited for the attempt was the hitherto unknown party militant Saddam Hussein, by now a law student in Baghdad. What happened next became part of Saddam's personal mythology, the topic of a government-sponsored novel and a film, *The Long Days*. In the cinematic version of the assassination attempt, the part of Saddam is played with verve by Saddam Kamel, his cousin and namesake, who somewhat resembled the Iraqi leader.

Hussein's Attempt to Assassinate Qassim

The assassination attempt on October 7, 1959, came close to success. Qassim was driving to a reception at the East German embassy. The Baath Party had a source inside the Defense Ministry who could tell them when Qassim would drive down al-Rashid Street, then Baghdad's main thoroughfare, with its white colonnades and luxury shops. Saddam's role was to provide covering fire for the four men who were to kill Qassim. Two of the gunmen were to open fire on anybody in the backseat while two aimed at the front. When the shooting started, Saddam became overexcited and drew the submachine gun he was hiding under a cloak given him by Khairallah Tulfah, his uncle. The assassins killed Qassim's driver, seriously wounded an aide, and hit Qassim himself in the shoulder. He was rushed to the hospital in a passing taxi. One of the attackers was shot dead, apparently by a chance shot from his own side. Saddam himself was hit in the fleshy part of his leg. "It was a very superficial wound to the shin," said the doctor who treated him. "A bullet just penetrated the skin and it stopped there in the shin of his leg. . . . During the night he cut it by using a razor blade and took the bullet out."

Years later Saddam told King Hussein [king of Jordan] that he had thought he would die after his failed attempt to kill Qassim. He gave lengthy and detailed accounts of his escape from the police, up the Tigris from Baghdad to Ouija. It was a critical element in his self-image as an Arab hero. . . .

Hussein's Exile Abroad

[After his failed assassination attempt, Hussein went into exile.] The three years Saddam spent in Damascus and Cairo were the only time in his life he lived abroad. Once he gained power, his visits to foreign countries were fleeting. Most of his time in exile was spent in Cairo under the protection of President [Gamal] Nasser, who was at odds with Qassim. Accounts of his behavior differ. Abdel Majid Farid, the secretary general of the Egyptian presidency, who had been an Egyptian military attaché in Baghdad until expelled, says: "We helped him go to the faculty of law and tried to get him an apartment. He was one of the leaders of the Iraqi Baath. He used to come to see me now and then to talk about developments in Baghdad. He was quiet, disciplined, and didn't ask for extra funds like the other exiles. He didn't have much interest in alcohol and girls."

This sounds a little too good to be true. Hussein Abdel Meguid, the owner of the Andiana Café, where Saddam used to meet with friends in the early 1960s, describes him as a troublemaker who did not pay his bills. "He would fight for any reason," he says. "We wanted to bar him from coming here. But the police came back and said he was protected by Nasser." Meguid says Saddam finally left owing the equivalent of several hundred dollars. . . .

Baath Party's CIA-Assisted 1963 Coup

On February 8, [1963,] a military coup in Baghdad, in which the Baath Party played a leading role, overthrew Qassim. Support for the conspirators was limited. In the first hours of fighting, they had only nine tanks under their control. The Baath Party had just 850 active members. But Qassim ignored warnings about the impending coup. What tipped the balance against him was the involvement of the United States. He had taken Iraq out of the anti-Soviet Baghdad Pact. In 1961, he threatened to occupy Kuwait and nationalized part of the Iraq Petroleum Company (IPC), the foreign oil consortium that exploited Iraq's oil.

In retrospect, it was the CIA's favorite coup. "We really had the *t*s crossed on what was happening," James Critchfield, then head of the CIA in the Middle East, told us. "We regarded it as a great victory." Iraqi participants later confirmed American involvement. "We came to power on a CIA train," admitted Ali Saleh Sa'adi, the Baath Party secretary general who was about to institute an unprecedented reign of terror. . . .

The triumph of the Baath Party was brief. It was deeply divided between its civilian and military wings. The new prime minister was Brigadier Ahmed Hassan al-Bakr, Saddam's cousin. Many of the other senior officers who overthrew Qassim were from Tikrit, though they belonged to a tribe different from that of al-Bakr and Saddam. There was little to hold the party together other than hatred of its enemies. In November, the new president, Abd al-Salaam Aref, first persuaded the military Baathists to turn on the civilian wing of their party and its militia. Soon afterward, Aref expelled the Baathist officers from the government.

Baath Party's 1968 Coup

Saddam played no role in the 1963 coup. It is not even clear that he took part in the massacres afterward. The following year he was jailed, but conditions were not onerous. The debacle of the Baathists' first bid for power put Saddam and al-Bakr in charge of the party. They planned to seize power again, avoiding the mistakes of 1963. The party was not strong enough to act on its own, but they suborned Abd al-Razzaq al-Nayif, the head of military intelligence. The coup took place on July 17, 1968, and, in contrast to what had happened five years before, this time it was the non-Baathist officers who were ousted within thirteen days of taking power.

Hussein's Rise to Power in Baath Party

Nine years after he tried to kill Qassim, Saddam was vice chairman of the Revolution Command Council (the RCC) and the second most powerful man in Iraq. The extent of his influence was kept deliberately shadowy. He was a civilian in what was, until the late seventies, primarily a military regime, with Ahmed Hassan al-Bakr as the president. In the 1970s, Saddam tried to ensure that army officers did not see foreign publications referring to him as "the new strongman of the regime." He seems to have assumed that they would not read Baath Party documents referring to them as "the military aristocracy." After the 1968 coup, the triumphant Baathists were as bloodthirsty as five years before, but their violence was more systematic. No opponent would get a second chance. Saddam took Nayif, the military intelligence chief who had assisted the Baathists in their coup and then been displaced, to the airport with his gun in Nayif's back. Even in exile, Nayif was considered a possible threat. In 1974, an assassin tried to kill him in his London apartment. Four years later, he was shot dead in a hotel in the same city. General Hardan al-Tikriti, the minister of defense, was dismissed in 1970 and was assassinated in Kuwait the following year. Previously, no regime in Iraq had been stable because army, party, tribe, and security services competed for power. Between 1968 and 1979, Saddam was able to get a grip on all four centers of power, which made him almost impossible to overthrow.

Saddam at this period had charm as well as ferocity. His attitude was very tribal, merciless and unforgiving to enemies, grateful and generous to friends. "There is no real mystery about the way we run Iraq," one of Saddam's associates once said. "We run it exactly as we used to run Tikrit." Saddam's rise was extraordinarily rapid. Less than ten years after he had fled for his life from Baghdad, he was the second most powerful man in Iraq. . . .

Hussein Becomes President

Saddam replaced al-Bakr as president in July 1979. The bloodbath with which he began his rule left no Iraqi in any doubt that all authority would in the future stem from him. This is important because it explains why nobody within the leadership tried to dissuade him from invading Iran in 1980 or Kuwait in 1990.

No criticism was allowed. This mattered less in terms of domestic Iraqi politics, where Saddam showed great skill. But in foreign affairs, his lack of experience and unwillingness to take advice was a recipe for disaster.

The opening moves in the crisis that led to the purge of the party were in early July 1979. President Bakr announced that he was to resign and hand over his office to Saddam at a meeting of the RCC on July 10. He said he was in poor health. But it rapidly emerged that there was strong opposition to Saddam among other leaders. Muhie Abdul-Hussein Mashhadi, the secretary of the ruling council, objected and demanded a vote on the decision. "It is inconceivable you should retire," he told Bakr. "If you are ill, why don't you take a rest?"

Saddam's opponents had waited too long to act. Muhie Abdul-Hussein Mashhadi was arrested for questioning and presumably tortured. Barzan, Saddam's half-brother, headed the investigation. In the next few days, Saddam toyed with those he was about to destroy. On July 18, party leaders were invited to a dinner party at the presidential palace. After the meal, they were each asked to write a detailed report of any meetings they might have had with Abdul-Hussein or another suspect, Mohammed Ayesh, the industry minister, the previous year. The circle of suspects increased. Barzan accused Ayesh of acting for Syria, Iraq's hated rival. In all, five members of the RCC, a quarter of its membership, were expelled. Along with sixteen others, they were executed on August 8. Branches of the Baath Party throughout Iraq each sent a delegate with a rifle to join the firing squad.

Saddam wanted the purge to create maximum terror and so ordered a videotape to be made of one of a series of meetings where he singled out those accused of conspiring against him. The tape indeed records a numbing and carefully orchestrated spectacle of terror. . . .

Hussein Enters the World Stage

It took a year for the significance of Saddam's takeover in Baghdad to become apparent to the rest of the Middle East. For the sixty years after Britain created Iraq, it was paralyzed by its own divisions. Despite growing oil wealth, it remained a third-rate power, unable to mobilize its resources. The purge of the Baath Party leadership in 1979 gave Saddam total control. He eliminated competitors for power within the party. He had already disposed of those outside. The long-running Kurdish rebellion, which had destabilized previous Iraqi governments, ended in 1975 when the shah of Iran with-

drew his support for the Iraqi Kurds in return for territorial concessions by Iraq. The country was growing wealthier. It produced 3.4
million barrels of oil a day and, after Saudi Arabia, had the largest
oil reserves in the Middle East.

Internal feuding in the 1960s and 1970s made Iraq a marginal
power in the Middle East and a very small player in world affairs.
Saddam now started on a sustained effort to win control of the Persian Gulf and leadership in the Arab world. His campaign had two
phases: The first began with his invasion of Iran in 1980 and ended
with Iraq's qualified victory eight years later. The second was much
shorter. Frustrated by what he saw as an attempt by Kuwait—backed
by the United States and Britain—to rob him of the fruits of his
victory over Iran by driving down the price of oil through overproduction, Saddam invaded the emirate on August 2, 1990. It was a
venture far beyond Iraq's political and military strength. The Americans and British were never likely to allow Iraq to win control of the
Gulf, which has 55 percent of the world's proven oil reserves.

In 1979, this final disaster lay far in the future.

The Iran-Iraq War

By Geoff Simons

Writer Geoff Simons describes in the following excerpt how the overthrow of the shah of Iran and the 1979 Islamic Revolution in that country ultimately led to a war between Iraq and Iran. Saddam Hussein feared that Iran's Shia Islamic revolutionaries would encourage Iraqi Shia Muslims to challenge his rule. As a result, Hussein attacked Iran in 1980, starting an eight-year war, from which Iraq emerged economically weakened but militarily strong. Simons also explains that, during the war and until Hussein invaded Kuwait in 1990, Iraq enjoyed massive military support from major states in the international community, including the United States. This placed the coalition forces during the Gulf War in the ironic position of fighting against the very military technology that they had recently supplied to Hussein.

[T]he Iran-Iraq conflict began when the Ayatollah] Khomeini came to power in Iran in February 1979 at the head of a revolutionary Islamic movement. Soon appeals were flooding from Tehran urging that Arab or state nationalism be abolished in Muslim lands in the interest of the higher unity of Islam. In an interview published in a Tehran newspaper, Khomeini declared: 'The Ummayad rule [661–750] was based on Arabism, the principle of promoting Arabs over all other peoples, which was an aim fundamentally opposed to Islam and its desire to abolish nationality and unite all mankind in a single community, under the aegis of a state indifferent to the matter of race and colour . . .'. The Ummayads, Khomeini claimed, were aiming 'to distort Islam completely by reviving the Arabism of the pre-Islamic age of ignorance, and the same aim is still pursued by the leaders of certain Arab countries who declare openly their desire to revive the Arabism of the Ummayads'. There is no doubt that by 'leaders of certain Arab countries', Khomeini had Saddam Hussein in mind: in a Paris interview in late 1978 Khomeini gave as his enemies: 'First, the Shah; then the American Satan; then Saddam Hussein and his infidel Ba'ath Party'.

Geoff Simons, *Iraq: From Sumer to Saddam*. New York: St. Martin's Press, 1994. Copyright © 1994 by Geoff Simons. Reproduced by permission of Palgrave Macmillan.

Hussein's Response

This theological offensive was not without effect of Saddam Hussein. He declared that the Islamic Revolution, or any other revolution that purported to be Islamic, 'must be a friend of the Arab revolution'; he began praying with greater frequency, at both Sunni and Shi'ite shrines; he made Imam Ali's [a Shia Muslim religious leader] birthday a national holiday; he resorted to the use of Islamic symbols; and resolved to 'fight injustice with the swords of the Imams', calling at the same time for 'a revival of heavenly values'. But there was no way of preventing a deepening of tension between the Iranian ayatollahs and the Iraqi Ba'athists, following the Khomeini revolution. Differences between the Sunnis and the Shi'ites were exacerbated, and immediately [after] Khomeini took power the new regime in Tehran began inciting the Iraqi Shi'ites to rise up against the Ba'ath government. Soon the Dawa, a Shi'ite party under Iranian influence, was plotting against the Iraqi regime, spreading pro-Iranian propaganda and organising a terrorist campaign. Saddam responded by putting the Ayatollah al-Sadr [leader of the Shia Muslims of Iraq] under house arrest in Najaf; Shi'ite riots followed in Baghdad, which were put down with great brutality. Then Saddam persuaded Bakr [leader of the 1963 Ba'ath coup and the first Ba'ath Party president] to resign and took over the presidency. After consolidating his position he completed the fearful purge of the Party and, in April 1980, had al-Sadr and his sister summarily hanged. Between 15,000 and 20,000 Shi'ites were expelled from Iraq, and hundreds more were arrested, tortured and executed. Saddam was already demonstrating that any threat to Iraq or to his own leadership would be met with the utmost severity. In a matter of months, using all the power of the security services that he had nurtured over the previous decade, he had secured his position.

In March 1980 the Iraqi authorities executed ninety-seven civilians and military men, half of them members of Dawa, now a banned organisation. Dawa activists then began attacking police stations, Ba'ath Party offices, and Popular Army recruiting centres. The repression of the Shi'ites continued. . . . Now border skirmishes between Iran and Iraq were happening at the rate of ten a month, and leading Iranian dissidents were being given radio stations in Iraq to beam anti-Khomeini propaganda into Iran. Washington staged an armed rescue attempt to retrieve the American hostages in Tehran, which failed dismally; and a pro-Shah coup attempt on 24–25 May was routed by Khomeini loyalists. A further coup attempt, staged by Shahpour Bakhtiar, the last premier under the Shah, was easily repulsed; and a fortnight later, on 27 July 1980, the last Shah of Iran died of cancer in Cairo. It was obvious to Saddam that he could not rely on Iranian monarchist generals or the imperialist United States to topple the Khomeini regime.

It seemed a propitious time for Saddam to intervene. There were constant reports of friction between the Iranian religious leaders and the then president Hassan Bani-Sadr; the Iranian army, following massive purges, was in disarray; arms had stopped flowing to Iran; and the country was diplomatically isolated. The 'great Satan' was incensed at the overthrow of its long-nurtured client and at the seizing of American hostages; and Tehran's Moscow links had collapsed following the Soviet invasion of Muslim Afghanistan. A friendless and chaotic Iran, starved of supplies and military expertise, seemed an easy target. The question was not whether Iraq should invade, but when.

By August 1980 Saddam Hussein had visited the rulers of Kuwait and Saudi Arabia, who said nothing to deflate his ambitions. Egypt had been suspended from the Arab League following the conclusion of the Egyptian accord with Israel, and there seemed to be a vacancy at the head of the Arab table. Saddam, now promised financial backing from Kuwait and Saudi Arabia, conscious of the deep hostilities between Iran and the United States, believed that he would be able to wage a brief and highly successful campaign. He would be greeted as a liberator by Arabs in Iranian territories and also by the Iranian Kurds struggling for recognition.

On 2 September 1980 Iraqi and Iranian troops clashed near Qasr-e Shirin, and soon afterwards Iranian artillery began shelling the Iraqi towns of Khanaqin and Mandali. On 6 September Iraq threatened to seize vast swathes of Iranian land in the Zain al Qaws region, supposedly granted to Iraq in [a] 1975 accord, if it was not ceded within a week. Iran responded with increased artillery fire, and Iraqi troops moved to capture a number of border posts. Saddam then claimed—in a televised speech to the National Assembly on 17 September—full control of the Shatt al-Arab, and heavy fighting broke out along the waterway. On 20 September Tehran called up reserves, and two days later Saddam's armies mounted a general offensive. What observers were later to call the 'first' Gulf War had begun. It would last for nearly a decade. . . .

Western Military Support for Hussein

Saddam Hussein, as a brutal master of domestic *realpolitik*, has now enjoyed more than two decades of effective power in Iraq: for a decade the powerful and scheming force behind the scenes, and for more than a decade as president. Throughout most of this period—

until 1990—he has been crucially supported by major states in the international community. The players have changed, sometimes moving off-stage, and then reappearing at a later time, according to the demands of business, the perceived self-interest of companies and countries, and the Cold War. But without the massive support—albeit spasmodic and fluctuating—provided over the years by Britain, France, West Germany, the United States, the Soviet Union and other countries, Saddam Hussein would never have been so well equipped for internal repression and for waging war against his neighbours.

When Iraq left the Baghdad Pact in 1958 the Soviet Union became Iraq's chief arms supplier, providing at that time such equipment as MiG-21 interceptors, TU-22 bombers and MiG-23 ground attack aircraft. The Iraqi-Soviet connection was briefly interrupted when the first Ba'ath government came to power in 1963, but then Soviet arms shipments were resumed for the rest of the 1960s. In 1972 Iraq was obtaining 95 percent of its arms equipment from the Soviet Union, a proportion that had diminished to 63 percent by 1979, with France a major supplier after 1975. By that time Iraq had decided to diversify its arms supply sources, as some gesture towards its status as a non-aligned state and as a way of avoiding undue dependence upon any one nation. At the same time France has established a posture of independence *vis-à-vis* NATO and was looking for new markets for arms sales. Iraq fitted the bill: it had oil money to spend. When Jacques Chirac was the French premier under the presidency of Valéry Giscard d'Estaing, France agreed to build an experimental nuclear plant outside Baghdad and to supply massive amounts of military equipment. In 1978 French contractors supplied eighteen Mirage F-1 interceptors and thirty helicopters, negotiated a deal for the production of the Mirage 200, and concluded a $2 billion deal for the supply of aircraft, tanks and other equipment. This support continued into the early 1980s; on 26 November 1982 President Mitterrand commented: 'We do not wish Iraq to be defeated in this war'. At this time Iraq was buying 40 percent of France's total armaments exports.

The French had welcomed these arms deals with open arms. When Prime Minister Jacques Chirac gave a press conference in Baghdad on 2 December 1974, after three days of talks with Saddam, the young French premier 'was exuberant', keen to talk of a 'veritable bonanza'. On 3 March 1975 Saddam met Chirac and Giscard d'Estaing in Paris and presented a long list of the weapons he wanted to purchase. Then Saddam flew to attend the OPEC conference in Algiers to agree the accord with the Shah, the controversial agreement that Saddam would later unilaterally abrogate. In early April he visited Moscow to agree a new arms deal and a nuclear co-operation pact with the Russians. Here Saddam secured a Soviet commitment for the training of Iraqi nuclear physicists and for the supply of a research reactor able to produce weapons-grade fuel; at the same time the Soviets demanded safeguards to prevent the production of nuclear weapons. In the 1960s the Arif government [1963–1968 Iraq government ruled by Colonel Arif and his brother] had purchased a modest nuclear reactor from the Soviet Union, and this formed the heart of the Thuwaitha nuclear research centre. When [Russian president Leonid] Brezhnev and [Minister Aleksey] Kosyg met Saddam in April 1975 they seemed reluctant to provide nuclear technology much in advance of the Thuwaitha beginnings, so again Saddam turned to France.

Hussein Provided with Nuclear Reactor

The French subsequently offered Saddam an Osiris research reactor and an Isis scale model, both of which were able to generate quantities of bomb-grade material. Both the systems were designed to operate on weapons-grade uranium, and a one-year supply amounted to 72 kilograms, enough for several Hiroshima-size atomic bombs. The reactor was at first called Osirak, but the two systems were later dubbed Tammuz I, and Tammuz II, after the Sumerian corn deity, lover of Ishtar (the Arabs' Athtar), who is brought back from the underworld to symbolise the eternity of the harvest. Saddam's intentions were clear. A few days after visiting the French Cadarache reactor he declared in an interview with the Lebanese weekly, *Al Usbu al-Arabi*: 'The agreement with France is the first concrete step towards the production of the Arab atomic weapon'. While the French were working on the Osirak reactors, Saddam was negotiating a ten-year nuclear co-operation pact with Brazil, who agreed to provide Iraq with large quantities of uranium, reactor technologies, equipment and training. Under the terms of this agreement, nuclear physicists from Iraq and Brazil were to 'exchange visits to research and development facilities'. The United States has claimed that Iraq also signed nuclear deals with India and China, though details have not been published. In 1978 the Italian nuclear body, Snia Techint, a subsidiary of Fiat, agreed to sell nuclear laboratories and other vital nuclear equipment to Iraq. According to Richard Wilson, director of the physics department at Harvard University, the 'Italian Project' was designed to facilitate the manufacture of a nuclear bomb.

When in April 1979 the French contractors had completed the manufacture of the Osirak reactor cores, the French Atomic Energy Commission (the CEA) made arrangements for them to be transported to the Mediterranean port of La Seyn-sur-Mer, to await an

Iraqi container ship. An American company, ORTEC (based at Oak Ridge, the home of the first US atomic bomb plant), had supplied a critical germanium detector, and the US company Hewlett-Packard had supplied computers. However, on the morning of 7 April there was an enormous explosion in the CNIM (Compagnie des Constructions navales et industrielles de la Méditerranée) warehouse where the nuclear equipment was stored. The reactor cores were completely destroyed but there was little other damage. A revelation in the German press a year later indicated that the attack (Operation Big Lift) had been staged by a seven-man Israeli commando group working for Mossad [Israeli Intelligence]. An enraged Saddam Hussein demanded that the French replace the reactors, and that they supply bomb-grade fuel. Eventually the French complied, the reactor was built, transported to Iraq, and set to go critical on 1 July 1981.

The nuclear fuel had been installed, the cooling channel was prepared, and suitable provisions had been made for plutonium production once the reactor began operation. The Iraqis were negotiating with NUKEM in West Germany for the supply of depleted uranium fuel pins, and Snia Techint was completing the last of the on-site reprocessing and fuel manufacturing laboratories. Iraqi agents had also concluded agreements with Niger, Brazil and Portugal for the supply of natural uranium ('yellowcake') for use in the Osirak system for the production of plutonium. In spring 1981 the International Atomic Energy Agency (IAEA) carried out its regular six-month inspection of the Thuwaitha plant, and publicly declared that all was well. However, Robert Richter, one of the IAEA inspectors, suggested that there were secret Thuwaitha facilities to which IAEA staff had not been given access. Other officials stated that his fears were groundless and he was subsequently fired from the Agency. Richter was not the only one to have anxieties. The Israeli prime minister Menachem Begin decided on drastic action; with the Israeli chief of staff, General Rafael Eitan, he began planning a scheme (Operation Babylon) for the bombing of the Osirak plant.

Israel Destroys Iraqi Nuclear Reactor

Begin authorised the building of a full-scale model of the Iraqi plant so that Israeli pilots could practise bombing it (it was remarked how closely the Osirak installation resembled Israel's own Dimona nuclear plant, also supplied by the French). On 7 June 1981 the Osirak facility was bombed by Israeli pilots flying F-16s and relying on American assistance. The CIA supplied the Israelis with satellite reconnaissance photographs that were vital to the success of the mission. The raid was skilfully planned. When the Israeli pilots were in

Jordanian airspace they conversed in Saudi-accented Arabic and informed Jordanian air controllers that they were a Saudi patrol gone astray; over Saudi Arabia they pretended to be Jordanians. The first wave of F-16s punched a hole in the reactor dome, after which a second wave of aircraft dropped 'dumb' (that is, not laser-guided) bombs with enough accuracy to destroy the reactor core, its containing walls, and the gantry crane.

The Israeli raid was almost universally condemned, with the new French premier, François Mitterrand, one of the first to protest. There were hundreds of French workers, and other foreign nationals, at the Tammuz plant when it was bombed; one Frenchman was killed. Mitterrand made a vague promise to rebuild the reactor, though few observers took his comments seriously. Washington's support for the raid was undisguised, with President Jimmy Carter later happy to admit US support for this and other controversial Israeli initiatives. In July 1981 Saudi Arabia announced that she would finance the rebuilding of the Iraqi reactor. But nothing came of this promise.

Both before and after the Osirak episode, Western support for Saddam Hussein continued unabated in one form or another. In 1981 French arms sales to Iraq were $2148 million; in 1982 $1925 million; and in 1983 $2000 million. Helicopters and Mirage F-1 fighter-bombers were being supplied, and France also agreed to lend Iraq five Super-Etendard aircraft equipped to carry Exocet air-to-surface missiles (these last arrived in Iraq in October 1983 and were returned to France two years later in accordance with the terms of the loan). A *Le Monde* estimate suggests that France sold Iraq arms to the value of $5.6 billion during the period of the 1980s Gulf War, and negotiated a further $4.7 billion-worth of civilian and commercial contracts.

US Military Aid to Iraq

In 1980 the US company General Electric received American approval to supply engines for Italian warships destined for the Iraqi navy, and in Baghdad a Lockheed sales team was negotiating the sale of helicopters to Saddam Hussein. In 1982 the Reagan administration decided to take Iraq off the list of countries branded as supporters of terrorism, even though it was well known that Saddam was providing refuge for Palestinian terrorists and committing other terrorist outrages. (In 1992, documents declassified under congressional pressure revealed that Iraqis' terrorist activities were well known at a time when the Reagan administration was asserting that there was no evidence to justify branding Iraq a terrorist state.) Full diplomatic relations were restored between Iraq and the United States in 1984, so preparing the way for an escalation of arms sales. In October 1983

William Eagleton, the top US official in Baghdad, suggested that the US should start supplying a wide range of equipment being denied to Iran: 'We can selectively lift restrictions on third-party transfers of US licensed military equipment to Iraq'. This could be done, he suggested, 'through Egypt'. The US also developed an arms interdiction plan (Operation Staunch) to prevent arms reaching Iran. This was a 'final piece of the tilt to Iraq' that the Senate Foreign Relations Committee noted in their 1984 report on US policy regarding the Iran-Iraq war.

In 1982 Washington had decided to clear the sale of 'civilian' transport aircraft to Iraq, and in June 1983 the Reagan administration authorised the supply to Iraq of sixty helicopters for 'agricultural use', machines that were obviously capable of conversion for military use. At the same time Washington provided credit of $460 million for the Iraqi purchase of 147,000 tonnes of American rice. This was an important gesture to Baghdad, boosting Iraqi morale at a time of economic hardship and signalling general US support for Saddam. It was acknowledged in Washington that an Iraqi defeat would be seen 'as a major blow to US interests'. In the autumn of 1983 a study by the US National Security Council reached this conclusion, and Washington decided to formulate plans 'to shore up Iraq morally and materially'. In March 1984 George Shultz commented that 'We wouldn't want to see' an Iranian victory, and so 'we have been deliberately working to improve our relationship with Iraq. . . . We have been co-operating with the Iraqis to a certain extent'. In January 1984 Washington branded Iran a terrorist nation, thus denying it access to US products, including arms; and made it plain to various countries—Britain, Israel, Italy, West Germany, Turkey, South Korea and others—that it did not want the supply of arms to Iran to continue.

The US also passed on surveillance information about the Gulf, collected by American-manned AWACS [Airborne Warning and Control Systems] to Riyadh [Saudi Arabia]—in full knowledge that the Saudis were transferring such data to Baghdad. This meant that the US was directly aiding the Iraqi management of the war, a fact later confirmed by Saddam. The Iran-Contra scandal [a scandal during the presidency of Ronald Reagan in which arms were sold to Iran with profits going to Nicaraguan contras] revealed that the US had been providing some illegal assistance to Iran but the pro-Iraqi 'tilt' remained, and survived the end of the war. In the summer of 1990, a few days before the invasion of Kuwait, the US State Department was trying to convince Congress to grant financial credits and other assistance to Iraq. And once the 1991 Gulf War was over, the extent of Western support for Saddam through the 1980s began to emerge.

Many countries were involved, but the lead players are those most vociferous in their current condemnation of the Iraqi regime. In the two years before the invasion of Kuwait, the United Kingdom was supplying Iraq with the Cymbeline [a radar product name] mortar-locating radar, spares for hovercraft and tanks, encryption equipment, and laser range-finders; France was supplying missiles, artillery pieces and attack helicopters; and the United States was supplying surveillance computers and avionics spares for naval equipment. The much-vaunted Coalition forces . . . , in seeking to expel Saddam from Kuwait, were forced to contend with a wide range of high-technology military equipment recently supplied by the leading Coalition states to Saddam.

Saddam Hussein's Chemical Attacks on the Kurds in the 1980s

By Human Rights Watch

The following is an excerpt from a report published in 1993 by Human Rights Watch, a nongovernmental organization based in the United States that is dedicated to investigating human rights abuses throughout the world. The selection describes a campaign of extermination against the Kurds of northern Iraq by the Saddam Hussein regime in the late 1980s. This campaign, known as Anfal, used various methods of repression and destruction, including the use of chemical weapons, to kill thousands of Kurdish civilians. The report concludes that the Iraqi regime committed the crime of genocide.

Anfal—"the Spoils"—is the name of the eighth *sura* [chapter] of the Koran. It is also the name given by the Iraqis to a series of military actions which lasted from February 23 until September 6, 1988. While it is impossible to understand the Anfal campaign without reference to the final phase of the 1980–1988 Iran-Iraq War, Anfal was not merely a function of that war. Rather, the winding-up of the conflict on Iraq's terms was the immediate historical circumstance that gave Baghdad the opportunity to bring to a climax its longstanding efforts to bring the Kurds to heel. For the Iraqi regime's anti-Kurdish drive dated back some fifteen years or more, well before the outbreak of hostilities between Iran and Iraq.

Anfal was also the most vivid expression of the "special powers" granted to Ali Hassan al-Majid, a cousin of President Saddam Hussein and secretary general of the Northern Bureau of Iraq's Ba'ath Arab Socialist Party. From March 29, 1987, until April 23, 1989, al-Majid was granted power that was equivalent, in Northern Iraq, to that of the President himself, with authority over all agencies of the state. Al-Majid, who is known to this day to Kurds as "Ali Anfal" or "Ali Chemical," was the overlord of the Kurdish genocide. Under his command, the central actors in Anfal were the First and Fifth Corps of the regular Iraqi Army, the General Security Directorate (*Mudiriyat al-Amn al-Ameh*) and Military Intelligence (*Istikhbarat*). The pro-government Kurdish militia known as the National Defense Battalions, or *jahsh*, assisted in important auxiliary tasks. But the integrated resources of the entire military, security and civilian apparatus of the Iraqi state were deployed, in al-Majid's words, "to solve the Kurdish problem and slaughter the saboteurs."

Human Rights Violations

The campaigns of 1987–1989 were characterized by the following gross violations of human rights:

• mass summary executions and mass disappearance of many tens of thousands of non-combatants, including large numbers of women and children, and sometimes the entire population of villages;

• the widespread use of chemical weapons, including mustard gas and the nerve agent GB, or Sarin, against the town of Halabja as well as dozens of Kurdish villages, killing many thousands of people, mainly women and children;

• the wholesale destruction of some 2,000 villages, which are described in government documents as having been "burned," "destroyed," "demolished" and "purified," as well as at least a dozen larger towns and administrative centers (*nahyas* and *qadhas*);

• the wholesale destruction of civilian objects by army engineers, including all schools, mosques, wells and other non-residential structures in the targeted villages, and a number of electricity substations;

• looting of civilian property and farm animals on a vast scale by army troops and pro-government militia;

• arbitrary arrest of all villagers captured in designated "prohibited areas" (*manateq al, mahdoureh*), despite the fact that these were their own homes and lands;

• arbitrary jailing and warehousing for months, in conditions of extreme deprivation, of tens of thousands of women, children and elderly people, without judicial order or any cause other than their presumed sympathies for the Kurdish opposition. Many hundreds of them were allowed to die of malnutrition and disease;

• forced displacement of hundreds of thousands of villagers upon

the demolition of their homes, their release from jail or return from exile; these civilians were trucked into areas of Kurdistan far from their homes and dumped there by the army with only minimal governmental compensation or none at all for their destroyed property, or any provision for relief, housing, clothing or food, and forbidden to return to their villages of origin on pain of death. In these conditions, many died within a year of their forced displacement;
   • destruction of the rural Kurdish economy and infrastructure.
   Like Nazi Germany, the Iraqi regime concealed its actions in euphemisms. Where Nazi officials spoke of "executive measures," "special actions" and "resettlement in the east," Ba'athist bureaucrats spoke of "collective measures," "return to the national ranks" and "resettlement in the south." But beneath the euphemisms, Iraq's crimes against the Kurds amount to genocide, [defined in the Convention on the Prevention and Punishment of the Crime of Genocide as] the "intent to destroy, in whole or in part, a national, ethnical, racial or religious group, as such.". . .

Expansion of Repression Against the Kurds

In the first three months after assuming his post as secretary general of the Ba'ath Party's Northern Bureau, Ali Hassan al-Majid began the process of definition of the group that would be targeted by Anfal, and vastly expanded the range of repressive activities against all rural Kurds. He decreed that "saboteurs" would lose their property rights, suspended the legal rights of all the residents of prohibited villages, and began ordering the execution of first-degree relatives of "saboteurs" and of wounded civilians whose hostility to the regime had been determined by the intelligence services.

   In June 1987, al-Majid issued two successive sets of standing orders that were to govern the conduct of the security forces through the Anfal campaign and beyond. These orders were based on the simple axiom on which the regime now operated: in the "prohibited" rural areas, all resident Kurds were coterminous with the *peshmerga* [members of the Kurdish nationalist guerrilla organization] insurgents, and they would be dealt with accordingly.

   The first of al-Majid's directives bans all human existence in the prohibited areas, to be applied through a shoot-to-kill policy. The second, numbered SF/4008, dated June 20, 1987, modifies and expands upon these orders. It constitutes a bald incitement to mass murder, spelled out in the most chilling detail. In clause 4, army commanders are ordered "to carry out random bombardments, using artillery, helicopters and aircraft, at all times of the day or night, in order to kill the largest number of persons present in these prohibited zones." In clause 5, al-Majid orders that, "All persons captured in those villages shall be detained and interrogated by the security services and those between the ages of 15 and 70 shall be executed after any useful information has been obtained from them, of which we should be duly notified."

Beginning of Chemical Attacks

Even as this legal and bureaucratic structure was being set in place, the Iraqi regime became the first in history to attack its own civilian population with chemical weapons. On April 15, 1987, Iraqi aircraft dropped poison gas on the KDP [Kurdish Democratic Party] headquarters at Zewa Shkan, close to the Turkish border in Dohuk governorate, and the PUK [Patriotic Union of Kurdistan] headquarters in the twin villages of Sergalou and Bergalou, in the governorate of Suleimaniyeh. The following afternoon, they dropped chemicals on the undefended civilian villages of Sheikh Wasan and Balisan, killing well over a hundred people, most of them women and children. Scores of other victims of the attack were abducted from their hospital beds in the city of Erbil, where they had been taken for treatment of their burns and blindness. They have never been seen again. These incidents were the first of at least forty documented chemical attacks on Kurdish targets over the succeeding eighteen months. They were also the first sign of the regime's new readiness to kill large numbers of Kurdish women and children indiscriminately.

Village Displacements

Within a week of the mid-April chemical weapons attacks, al-Majid's forces were ready to embark upon what he described as a three-stage program of village clearances or collectivization. The first ran from April 21 to May 20; the second from May 21 to June 20. More than 700 villages were burned and bulldozed, most of them along the main highways in government-controlled areas. The third phase of the operation, however, was suspended; with Iraqi forces still committed to the war front, the resources required for such a huge operation were not available. But the goals of the third stage would eventually be accomplished by Anfal.

Census Targeting

In terms of defining the target group for destruction, no single administrative step was more important to the Iraqi regime than the national census of October 17, 1987. Now that the springtime village clearances had created a virtual buffer strip between the government and the *peshmerga*-controlled zones, the Ba'ath Party offered the inhabitants of the prohibited areas an ultimatum: either they could "return to the national ranks"—in other words, abandon their homes and livelihoods and accept compulsory relocation in a squalid camp under the eye of the security forces; or they could lose their Iraqi citizenship and be regarded as military deserters. The second option was tantamount to a death sentence, since the census legislation made those who refused to be counted subject to an August 1987 decree of the ruling Revolutionary Command Council, imposing the death penalty on deserters.

In the period leading up to the census, al-Majid refined the target group further. He ordered his intelligence officials to prepare detailed case-by-case dossiers of "saboteurs'" families who were still living in the government-controlled areas. When these dossiers were complete, countless women, children and elderly people were forcibly transferred to the rural areas to share the fate of their *peshmerga* relatives. This case-by-case, family-by-family sifting of the population was to become a characteristic feature of the decisions made during the Anfal period about who should live and who should die.

Last, but not without significance, the census gave those who registered only two alternatives when it came to declaring their nationality. One could either be Arab or Kurdish—a stipulation that was to have the direst consequences for other minority groups, such as the Yezidis, Assyrians and Chaldean Christians who continued to live in the Kurdish areas.

Military Action Against the Kurds

The Anfal campaign began four months after the census, with a massive military assault on the PUK headquarters at Sergalou-Bergalou on the night of February 23, 1988. Anfal would have eight stages in all, seven of them directed at areas under the control of the PUK. The KDP-controlled areas in the northwest of Iraqi Kurdistan, which the regime regarded as a lesser threat, were the target of the Final Anfal operation in late August and early September 1988.

The Iraqi authorities did nothing to hide the campaign from public view. On the contrary, as each phase of the operation triumphed, its successes were trumpeted with the same propaganda fanfare that attended the victorious battles in the Iran-Iraq War. Even today, Anfal is celebrated in the official Iraqi media. The fifth anniversary in 1993 of the fall of Sergalou and Bergalou on March 19, 1988, was the subject of banner headlines.

Iraqi troops tore through rural Kurdistan with the motion of a gigantic windshield wiper, sweeping first clockwise, then counter-clockwise, through one after another of the "prohibited areas." The First Anfal, centered on the siege of the PUK headquarters, took more than three weeks. Subsequent phases of the campaign were generally shorter, with a brief pause between each as army units moved on to the next target. The Second Anfal, in the Qara Dagh region, lasted from March 22 to April 1, 1988; the Third, covering the hilly plain known as Germian, took from April 7 to April 20; the Fourth, in the valley of the Lesser Zab river, was the shortest of all, lasting only from May 3 to May 8.

Only in the Fifth Anfal, which began on May 15 in the mountainous region northeast of Erbil, did the troops have any real difficulty in meeting their objectives. Encountering fierce resistance in difficult terrain from the last of the PUK *peshmerga,* the regime called a temporary halt to the offensive on June 7. On orders from the Office of the Presidency (indicating the personal supervisory role that Saddam Hussein himself played in Anfal), the operation was renewed twice in July and August, with these actions denominated Anfal VI and Anfal VII. Eventually, on August 26, the last PUK-controlled area was declared "cleansed of saboteurs."

By this time, Iran had accepted Iraq's terms for a ceasefire to end the war, freeing up large numbers of Iraqi troops to carry the Anfal operation into the Badinan area of northern Iraqi Kurdistan. The Final Anfal began at first light on August 25, and was over in a matter of days. On September 6, 1988, the Iraqi regime made its de facto declaration of victory by announcing a general amnesty for all Kurds. (Ali Hassan al-Majid later told aides that he had opposed the amnesty, but had gone along with it as a loyal party man.)

Pattern of Chemical Attacks

Each stage of Anfal followed roughly the same pattern. It characteristically began with chemical attacks from the air on both civilian and *peshmerga* targets, accompanied by a military blitz against PUK or KDP military bases and fortified positions. The deadly cocktail of mustard and nerve gases was much more lethal against civilians than against the *peshmerga,* some of whom had acquired gas masks and other rudimentary defenses. In the village of Sayw Senan (Second Anfal), more than eighty civilians died; in Goktapa (Fourth Anfal), the death toll was more than 150; in Wara (Fifth Anfal) it was thirty-seven. In the largest chemical attack of all, the March 16 bombing of the Kurdish town of Halabja, between 3,200 and 5,000 residents died. As a city, Halabja was not technically part of Anfal—the raid was carried out in reprisal for its capture by *peshmerga* supported by Iranian Revolutionary Guards—but it was very much part of the Kurdish genocide.

After the initial assault, ground troops and *jahsh* [pro-government Kurdish militia] enveloped the target area from all sides, destroying all human habitation in their path, looting household possessions and farm animals and setting fire to homes, before calling in demolition crews to finish the job. . . . Convoys of army trucks stood by to transport the villagers to nearby holding centers and transit camps, while the *jahsh* combed the hillsides to track down anyone who had escaped. (Some members of the militia, an asset of dubious reliability to the regime, also saved thousands of lives by spiriting people away to safety or helping them across army lines.) Secret police combed the towns, cities and complexes to hunt down Anfal fugitives, and in several cases lured them out of hiding with false offers of amnesty and a "return to the national ranks"—a promise that now concealed a more sinister meaning. . . .

Continued Repression of the Kurds

Although Anfal as a military campaign ended with the general amnesty of September 6, 1988, its logic did not. Those who were released from prisons such as Nugra Salman, Dibs and Salamiyeh, as well as those who returned from exile under the amnesty, were relocated to complexes with no compensation and no means of support. Civilians who tried to help them were hunted down by *Amn* [Iraq's General Security Directorate]. The *mujamma'at* [crude new settlements built for relocation of Kurds] that awaited the survivors of the Final Anfal in Badinan were places of residence in name alone; the *Anfalakan* [Kurds who were victims of the Anfal campaign] were merely dumped on the barren earth of the Erbil plain with no infrastructure other than a perimeter fence and military guard towers. Here, hundreds perished from disease, exposure, hunger or malnutrition, and the after-effects of exposure to chemical weapons. Several hundreds more—non-Muslim Yezidis, Assyrians and Chaldeans, including many women and children—were abducted from the camps and disappeared, collateral victims of the Kurdish genocide. Their particular crime was to have remained in the prohibited majority Kurdish areas after community leaders declined to accept the regime's classification of them as Arabs in the 1987 census.

The regime had no intention of allowing the amnestied Kurds to exercise their full civil rights as Iraqi citizens. They were to be deprived of political rights and employment opportunities until *Amn* certified their loyalty to the regime. They were to sign written pledges that they would remain in the *mujamma'at* to which they had been assigned—on pain of death. They were to understand that the prohibited areas remained off limits and were often sown with landmines to discourage resettlement; directive SF/4008, and in particular clause 5, with its order to kill all adult males, would remain in force and would be carried out to the letter.

Arrests and executions continued, some of the latter even involving prisoners who were alive, in detention, at the time of the amnesty. Middle East Watch has documented three cases of mass executions in late 1988; in one of them, 180 people were put to death. Documents from one local branch of *Amn* list another eighty-seven executions in the first eight months of 1989, one of them a man accused of "teaching the Kurdish language in Latin script."

The few hundred Kurdish villages that had come through Anfal unscathed as a result of their pro-government sympathies had no guarantees of lasting survival, and dozens more were burned and bulldozed in late 1988 and 1989. Army engineers even destroyed the large Kurdish town of Qala Dizeh (population 70,000) and declared its environs a "prohibited area," removing the last significant population center close to the Iranian border.

Killing, torture and scorched-earth policies continued, in other words, to be a matter of daily routine in Iraqi Kurdistan, as they always had been under the rule of the Ba'ath Arab Socialist Party. But the Kurdish problem, in al-Majid's words, had been solved; the "saboteurs" had been slaughtered. Since 1975, some 4,000 Kurdish villages had been destroyed; at least 50,000 rural Kurds had died in Anfal alone, and very possibly twice that number; half of Iraq's productive farmland had been laid waste. All told, the total number of Kurds killed over the decade [since a revolt in the 1970s led by Kurdish fighter Mullah Mustafa Barzani] . . . is well into six figures.

Genocide Completed

By April 23, 1989, the Ba'ath Party felt that it had accomplished its goals, for on that date it revoked the special powers that had been granted to Ali Hassan al-Majid two years earlier. At a ceremony to greet his successor, the supreme commander of Anfal made it clear that "the exceptional situation is over."

To use the language of the Genocide Convention, the regime's aim had been to *destroy the group* (Iraqi Kurds) *in part*, and it had done so. Intent and act had been combined, resulting in the consummated crime of genocide.

The Gulf War to Liberate Kuwait

By George H.W. Bush

On August 2, 1990, Saddam Hussein invaded Kuwait after accusing it of driving down the price of oil by cheating on OPEC (Organization of Petroleum Exporting Countries) quotas and flooding the market, thwarting Hussein's attempts to rebuild Iraq's economy after the Iran-Iraq War. When Iraq refused to withdraw from Kuwait despite United Nations–imposed economic sanctions, the United States led an allied military attack against targets in Iraq and Kuwait. The following is the address given to the nation by U.S. president George H.W. Bush in January 1991 announcing the launching of the attack, called "Operation Desert Storm." In the speech, President Bush outlines the objectives of the military operation, which included the destruction of Iraqi military arsenals (including nuclear and chemical facilities) and the liberation of Kuwait. He also explains the timing of the military action and defines a "new world order" in which UN rule of law would govern the conduct of nations.

J ust 2 hours ago, [on January 16, 1991,] allied air forces began an attack on military targets in Iraq and Kuwait [called "Operation Desert Storm"]. These attacks continue as I speak. Ground forces are not engaged.

This conflict started August 2d when the dictator of Iraq invaded a small and helpless neighbor. Kuwait—a member of the Arab League and a member of the United Nations—was crushed; its people brutalized. Five months ago, Saddam Hussein started this cruel war against Kuwait. Tonight, the battle has been joined.

This military action, taken in accord with UN resolutions—and with the consent of the United States Congress—follows months of constant and virtually endless diplomatic activity on the part of the United Nations, the United States, and many, many other countries.

George H.W. Bush, address to the nation, January 16, 1991.

Arab leaders sought what became known as an Arab solution—only to conclude that Saddam Hussein was unwilling to leave Kuwait. Others traveled to Baghdad in a variety of efforts to restore peace and justice. Our Secretary of State, James Baker, held a historic meeting in Geneva—only to be totally rebuffed. This past weekend, in a last-ditch effort, the Secretary General of the United Nations went to the Middle East, with peace in his heart—his second such mission. And he came back from Baghdad with no progress at all in getting Saddam Hussein to withdraw from Kuwait.

Now the 28 countries with forces in the Gulf area have exhausted all reasonable efforts to reach a peaceful resolution; [we] have no choice but to drive Saddam from Kuwait by force. We will not fail.

War Objectives

As I report to you, air attacks are underway against military targets in Iraq. We are determined to knock out Saddam Hussein's nuclear bomb potential. We will also destroy his chemical weapons facilities. Much of Saddam's artillery and tanks will be destroyed. Our operations are designed to best protect the lives of all the coalition forces by targeting Saddam's vast military arsenal. Initial reports from [Desert Storm forces commander] General Schwarzkopf are that our operations are proceeding according to plan.

Our objectives are clear. Saddam Hussein's forces will leave Kuwait. The legitimate government of Kuwait will be restored to its rightful place, and Kuwait will once again be free. Iraq will eventually comply with all relevant UN resolutions. And then, when peace is restored, it is our hope that Iraq will live as a peaceful and cooperative member of the family of nations, thus, enhancing the security and stability of the Gulf.

Why Act Now?

Some may ask, why act now? Why not wait? The answer is clear: The world could wait no longer. Sanctions, though having some effect, showed no signs of accomplishing their objective. Sanctions were tried for well over 5 months, and we and our allies concluded that sanctions alone would not force Saddam from Kuwait.

While the world waited, Saddam Hussein systematically raped, pillaged, and plundered a tiny nation, no threat to his own. He subjected the people of Kuwait to unspeakable atrocities—and among those maimed and murdered, innocent children.

While the world waited, Saddam sought to add to the chemical weapons arsenal he now possesses an infinitely more dangerous weapon of mass destruction—a nuclear weapon.

And while the world waited, while the world talked peace and withdrawal, Saddam Hussein dug in and moved massive forces into Kuwait.

While the world waited, while Saddam stalled, more damage was being done to the fragile economies of the Third World, the emerging democracies of Eastern Europe, to the entire world including to our own economy.

The United States, together with the United Nations, exhausted every means at our disposal to bring this crisis to a peaceful end. However, Saddam clearly felt that by stalling and threatening and defying the United Nations, he could weaken the forces arrayed against him.

While the world waited, Saddam Hussein met every overture of peace with open contempt. While the world prayed for peace, Saddam prepared for war.

I had hoped that when the US Congress, in historic debate, took its resolute action, Saddam would realize he could not prevail and would move out of Kuwait in accord with the UN resolutions. He did not do that. Instead, he remained intransigent, certain that time was on his side.

Saddam was warned over and over again to comply with the will of the United Nations. Leave Kuwait or be driven out. Saddam has arrogantly rejected all warnings. Instead, he tried to make this a dispute between Iraq and the United States of America.

Well, he failed. Tonight, 28 nations—countries from five continents: Europe and Asia, Africa, and the Arab League—have forces in the Gulf area standing shoulder-to-shoulder against Saddam Hussein. These countries had hoped the use of force could be avoided. Regrettably, we now believe that only force will make him leave.

New World Order

Prior to ordering our forces into battle, I instructed our military commanders to take every necessary step to prevail as quickly as possible and with the greatest degree of protection possible for American and allied servicemen and women. I've told the American people before that this will not be another Vietnam. And I repeat this here tonight. Our troops will have the best possible support in the entire world, and they will not be asked to fight with one hand tied behind their backs.

I'm hopeful that this fighting will not go on for long and that casualties will be held to an absolute minimum.

This is a historic moment. We have, in this past year, made great progress in ending the long era of conflict and Cold War. We have before us the opportunity to forge, for ourselves and for future generations, a new world order—a world where the rule of law, not the law of the jungle, governs the conduct of nations.

When we are successful—and we will be—we have a real chance at this new world order—an order in which a credible United Nations can use its peacekeeping role to fulfill the promise and vision of the UN's founders.

Prayers for Peace

We have no argument with the people of Iraq—indeed, for the innocents caught in this conflict, I pray for their safety.

Our goal is not the conquest of Iraq; it is the liberation of Kuwait. It is my hope that somehow the Iraqi people can, even now, convince their dictator that he must lay down his arms, leave Kuwait, and let Iraq itself rejoin the family of peace-loving nations.

Thomas Paine wrote many years ago: "These are the times that try men's souls." Those well-known words are so very true today. But even as planes of the multinational forces attack Iraq, I prefer to think of peace, not war. I am convinced not only that we will prevail but that out of the horror of combat will come the recognition that no nation can stand against a world united. No nation will be permitted to brutally assault its neighbor.

No president can easily commit our sons and daughters to war. They are the nation's finest. Ours is an all volunteer force—magnificently trained, highly motivated. The troops know why they're there. And listen to what they say, for they've said it better than any president or prime minister ever could.

Listen to "Hollywood" Huddleston, Marine Lance Corporal. He says, "Let's free these people so we can go home and be free again." He's right. The terrible crimes and tortures committed by Saddam's henchmen against the innocent people of Kuwait are an affront to mankind and a challenge to the freedom of all.

Listen to one of our great officers out there, Marine Lieutenant General Walter Boomer. He said, "There are things worth fighting for. A world in which brutality and lawlessness are allowed to go unchecked isn't the kind of world we're going to want to live in."

Listen to Master Sergeant J.P. Kendall of the 82nd Airborne. "We're here for more than just the price of a gallon of gas. What we're doing is going to chart the future of the world for the next hundred years. It's better to deal with this guy now than 5 years from now."

And finally, we should all sit up and listen to Jackie Jones, an Army Lieutenant, when she says, "If we let him get away with this, who knows what's going to be next?"

I have called upon "Hollywood" and Walter and J.P. and Jackie and all their courageous comrades in arms to do what must be done. Tonight, America and the world are deeply grateful to them and to their families. And let me say to everyone listening or watching tonight: When the troops we've sent in finish their work, I am determined to bring them home as soon as possible.

Tonight, as our forces fight, they and their families are in our prayers. May God bless each and every one of them and the coalition forces at our side in the Gulf—and may He continue to bless our nation, the United States of America.

CHAPTER 2

The U.S. War Against Iraq and Its Aftermath

America Declares War on Iraq

By George W. Bush

Part of the condition for ending the Persian Gulf War in 1991 was that Iraq destroy all of its weapons of mass destruction. UN weapons inspectors were sent to verify compliance with this conition, but in many occasions Iraq was accused of not cooperating with them. The weapons inspectors were eventually pulled out. A new team of UN weapons inspectors, called the UN Monitoring, Verification and Inspection Commission (UNMOVIC), returned to Iraq in late November 2002, along with inspectors from the International Atomic Energy Agency (IAEA). Although UNMOVIC and IAEA failed to find any weapons of mass destruction, Iraq displayed a lack of full cooperation with UN inspection demands by not accounting for weapons that remained after the inspections in the 1990s. As a result, the United States and Britain sought to obtain support in the UN for a second resolution authorizing military action against Iraq.

However, significant opposition to war developed in many countries, most notably France, Germany, Russia, and China—all members of the UN Security Council. These nations urged that weapons inspections be given more time to work. The United States, therefore, was unable to secure the necessary votes for the second resolution, and it feared that France might well veto any such resolution. Instead, the United States, together with its ally Britain, decided to attack Iraq without specific authorization from the UN. In the following selection, originally given as a speech to the nation on March 17, 2003, President George W. Bush announces U.S. war plans. In the speech, Bush explains that the war is necessary to depose Iraqi leader Saddam Hussein and rid the nation of weapons of mass destruction. The campaign, he argues, is necessary to protect U.S. national security. The U.S./British attack on Iraq began during the night of March 19, 2003.

George W. Bush, televised address to the nation, March 17, 2003.

M y fellow citizens, events in Iraq have now reached the final days of decision.

For more than a decade, the United States and other nations have pursued patient and honorable efforts to disarm the Iraqi regime without war. That regime pledged to reveal and destroy all its weapons of mass destruction as a condition for ending the Persian Gulf war in 1991. Since then the world has engaged in 12 years of diplomacy. We have passed more than a dozen resolutions in the United Nations Security Council. We have sent hundreds of weapons inspectors to oversee the disarmament of Iraq. Our good faith has not been returned.

The Danger from Iraq Is Clear

The Iraqi regime has used diplomacy as a ploy to gain time and advantage. It has uniformly defied Security Council resolutions demanding full disarmament. Over the years, U.N. weapon inspectors have been threatened by Iraqi officials, electronically bugged and systematically deceived. Peaceful efforts to disarm the Iraqi regime have failed again and again because we are not dealing with peaceful men. Intelligence gathered by this and other governments leaves no doubt that the Iraq regime continues to possess and conceal some of the most lethal weapons ever devised.

This regime has already used weapons of mass destruction against Iraq's neighbors and against Iraq's people. The regime has a history of reckless aggression in the Middle East. It has a deep hatred of America and our friends. And it has aided, trained and harbored terrorists, including operatives of Al Qaeda.

The danger is clear. Using chemical, biological or, one day, nuclear weapons, obtained with the help of Iraq, the terrorists could fulfill their stated ambitions and kills thousands or hundreds of thousands of innocent people in our country or any other.

The United States and other nations did nothing to deserve or invite this threat, but we will do everything to defeat it. Instead of drifting along toward tragedy, we will set a course toward safety. Before the day of horror can come, before it is too late to act, this danger will be removed.

The United States Has Authority to Use Force

The United States of America has the sovereign authority to use force in assuring its own national security.

Recognizing the threat to our country, the United States Congress voted overwhelmingly [in 2002] to support the use of force against

Iraq. America tried to work with the United Nations to address this threat because we wanted to resolve the issue peacefully. We believe in the mission of the United Nations. One reason the U.N. was founded after the Second World War was to confront aggressive dictators actively and early before they can attack the innocent and destroy the peace.

In the case of Iraq, the Security Council did act in the early 1990's. Under Resolutions 678 and 687, both still in effect, the United States and our allies are authorized to use force in ridding Iraq of weapons of mass destruction. This is not a question of authority, it is a question of will.

Last September [2002], I went to the U.N. General Assembly and urged the nations of the world to unite and bring an end to this danger. On Nov. 8, the Security Council unanimously passed Resolution 1441 finding Iraq in material breach of its obligations and vowing serious consequences if Iraq did not fully and immediately disarm. Today, no nation can possibly claim that Iraq has disarmed, and it will not disarm so long as Saddam Hussein holds power.

For the last four and a half months [November 2002–March 2003], the United States and our allies have worked within the Security Council to enforce that council's longstanding demands. Yet some permanent members of the Security Council have publicly announced that they will veto any resolution that compels the disarmament of Iraq. These governments share our assessment of the danger, but not our resolve to meet it.

Many nations, however, do have the resolve and fortitude to act against this threat to peace. And a broad coalition is now gathering to enforce the just demands of the world. The United Nations Security Council has not lived up to its responsibilities, so we will rise to ours.

Saddam Hussein Must Leave Iraq or Face War

In recent days, some governments in the Middle East have been doing their part. They have delivered public and private messages urging the dictator to leave Iraq so that disarmament can proceed peacefully. He has thus far refused. All the decades of deceit and cruelty have now reached an end. Saddam Hussein and his sons must leave Iraq within 48 hours. Their refusal to do so will result in military conflict, commenced at a time of our choosing. For their own safety, all foreign nationals, including journalists and inspectors should leave Iraq immediately.

Many Iraqis can hear me tonight in a translated radio broadcast.

And I have a message for them. If we must begin a military campaign, it will be directed against the lawless men who rule your country and not against you. As our coalition takes away their power we will deliver the food and medicine you need. We will tear down the apparatus of terror. And we will help you to build a new Iraq that is prosperous and free.

In a free Iraq there will be no more wars of aggression against your neighbors, no more poison factories, no more executions of dissidents, no more torture chambers and rape rooms. The tyrant will soon be gone. The day of your liberation is near.

It is too late for Saddam Hussein to remain in power. It is not too late for the Iraqi military to act with honor and protect your country by permitting the peaceful entry of coalition forces to eliminate weapons of mass destruction. Our forces will give Iraqi military units clear instructions on actions they can take to avoid being attacked and destroyed.

I urge every member of the Iraqi military and intelligence services, if war comes, do not fight for a dying regime that is not worth your own life. And all Iraqi military and civilian personnel should listen carefully to this warning. In any conflict your fate will depend on your actions. Do not destroy oil wells, a source of wealth that belongs to the Iraqi people. Do not obey any command to use weapons of mass destruction against anyone, including the Iraqi people. War crimes will be prosecuted. War criminals will be punished. And it will be no defense to say I was just following orders.

Should Saddam Hussein choose confrontation, the American people can know that every measure has been taken to avoid war. And every measure will be taken to win it. Americans understand the cost of conflict because we have paid them in the past. War has no certainty except the certainty of sacrifice. Yet the only way to reduce the harm and duration of war is to apply the full force and might of our military. And we are prepared to do so.

The Risk of Terrorist Attacks

If Saddam Hussein attempts to cling to power, he will remain a deadly foe until the end. In desperation he and terrorist groups might try to conduct terrorist operations against the American people and our friends. These attacks are not inevitable. They are, however, possible. And this very fact underscores the reason we cannot live under the threat of blackmail.

The terrorist threat to America and the world will be diminished the moment that Saddam Hussein is disarmed. Our government is on heightened watch against these dangers. Just as we are preparing to ensure victory in Iraq, we are taking further actions to protect our homeland. In recent days American authorities have expelled from the country certain individuals with ties to Iraqi intelligence services. Among other measures I have directed additional security at our airports and increased Coast Guard patrols of major seaports.

The Department of Homeland Security is working closely with the nation's governors to increase armed security at critical facilities across America. Should enemies strike our country they would be attempting to shift our attention with panic and weaken our morale with fear. In this they would fail. No act of theirs can alter the course or shake the resolve of this country. We are a peaceful people, yet we're not a fragile people, and we will not be intimidated by thugs and killers. If our enemies dare to strike us, they and all who have aided them will face fearful consequences.

U.S. Action Is Necessary to Prevent a Threat

We are now acting because the risks of inaction would be far greater. In one year or five years the power of Iraq to inflict harm on all flee nations would be multiplied many times over. With these capabilities, Saddam Hussein and his terrorist allies could choose the moment of deadly conflict when they are strongest. We choose to meet that threat now where it arises before it can appear suddenly in our skies and cities.

The cause of peace requires all free nations to recognize new and undeniable realities. In the 20th century some chose to appease murderous dictators whose threats were allowed to grow into genocide and global war. In this century when evil men plot chemical, biological and nuclear terror, a policy of appeasement could bring destruction of a kind never before seen on this earth. Terrorists and terrorist states do not reveal these threats with fair notice in formal declarations. And responding to such enemies only after they have struck first is not self-defense, it is suicide. The security of the world requires disarming Saddam Hussein now.

As we enforce the just demands of the world, we will also honor the deepest commitments of our country. Unlike Saddam Hussein, we believe the Iraqi people are deserving and capable of human liberty. And when the dictator has departed, they can set an example to all the Middle East of a vital and peaceful and self-governing nation.

The United States with other countries will work to advance liberty and peace in that region. Our goal will not be achieved overnight. But it can come over time. The power and appeal of human liberty is felt in every life and every land. And the greatest power of freedom is to overcome hatred and violence, and turn the creative gifts of men and women to the pursuits of peace. That is the future we choose. Free nations have a duty to defend our people by uniting against the violent. And tonight, as we have done before, America and our allies accept that responsibility.

Good night and may God continue to bless America.

The Iraq War Was a Great Success

By the *National Review*

The following editorial, written by the editors of the National Review, *praises the American military victory in Iraq. As the editors point out, a mere three weeks of war freed Iraqis and the world from the tyranny of Saddam Hussein. Critics of the war who warned of large numbers of American casualties and a military quagmire look foolish in hindsight. Instead, U.S. forces suffered relatively few casualties, and the war demonstrated American military power to other potentially dangerous dictators in other parts of the world. According to this editorial, the war showed that America's response to the September 11, 2001, terrorist attacks was not revenge but a positive effort to liberate Afghanistan and Iraq from horrible tyrannies.*

The editors, however, urge the United States to stay engaged in Iraq and in changing the political order in the Middle East. U.S. forces must search for and destroy weapons of mass destruction, continue the war against terrorism, and begin the process of bringing order and governance to Iraq. Looting must be stopped, Iraqi debts forgiven, and sanctions lifted. In addition, plans must be made for the creation of a nontotalitarian government in Iraq and for eventually building a new Iraqi military.

S addam Hussein's regime is dead, as the man himself may be. Three weeks of war freed Iraqis from his tyranny, and the region and the world from the threat it posed. Our coalition has suffered only 154 casualties. Dictators from Damascus to Pyongyang are newly fearful of American power and resolve. And we are confident that the dead regime's weapons of mass destruction will soon be found and destroyed. This is a victory in which President [George W.] Bush, Prime Ministers [Tony] Blair and [John] Howard, our armed forces, and the people of America, Britain, and Australia take pride. As Brink Lindsey noted on his website, America's response to the brutal murder of its citizens [during the September 11, 2001, terrorist attacks] was not to strike out blindly for revenge. It was "to liberate 50 million people in Afghanistan and Iraq from two of the most hideous tyrannies on earth."

Opponents of the war are now saying that they never doubted that it would be won so easily. But this is simply untrue. Politicians, journalists, and retired generals opposed to the war made inflated projections of bodybags coming home. The risk of war for American troops was, indeed, the most popular argument that opponents of the war made. The idea that we were in a quagmire was also the point they made most relentlessly once the fighting had started. They were foolish then, and they look it now. Some of these people made the same predictions before the first Gulf War; they clearly do not learn from experience. But the rest of us should know not to trust their judgment in future foreign-policy controversies.

Challenges Ahead

Those controversies are already coming upon us. Although we have won a great victory, this is not a moment for resting on laurels. We still have to find and destroy the regime's weapons of mass destruction. The war on terrorism is still going on, and we face many challenges—and temptations. The public may be tempted to believe that we can return to pre-9/11 normalcy, and the Bush administration may be tempted to think that it should now turn its attention almost exclusively to domestic issues. We hope that the president will soon make a prime-time address making it clear that these temptations will be resisted. We are not, and should not be, looking for new military battles to fight. But we do need to remain engaged in changing the political order of the Middle East.

The immediate challenge is, of course, to bring order and governance to Iraq, followed by humanitarian assistance and reconstruction aid. Some looting and chaos following the Ba'athist regime's collapse was to be expected, and is not a black mark on America's record. But it needs to be brought to an end. The debts incurred by the old regime should be voided, and sanctions lifted. The State Department and the CIA continue to snipe at Ahmad Chalabi, an Iraqi democratic leader, claiming that he lacks popular support (something that is indisputably true of the various generals and thugs whom the CIA has preferred to Chalabi). Nobody is suggesting that America install Chalabi or an associate in power. But he and other democratic leaders should be given the chance to prove themselves, to demonstrate and build whatever support they can. We should welcome help from other countries and even from the United Nations, so long as they do not interfere with a process of democratization for which many of them lack enthusiasm.

We should also reject the fantasy, popular in some quarters, of a permanently demilitarized Iraq. We want a free Iraq to be a peaceful one, but it is in a tough neighborhood and will need to be able to defend itself

The Larger Challenges

The larger challenge is to create a new, non-totalitarian political order in the Mideast. We may be able to exert a positive influence on the region through forms of pressure short of war, the exemplary force of our operation in Iraq, and, we hope, the spillover effects of Iraqi liberalization. The tough rhetoric from the Bush administration toward Syria is a welcome sign that we intend to use the troops we have parked next door to modify its behavior. At the same time, it may be wise to demonstrate that we have no relish for occupying Arab states by quitting Saudi Arabia. The strategic logic of our troop presence there no longer applies.

Many Americans, and even more Britishers and Europeans, believe that solving the Israeli-Palestinian conflict should also be on our agenda. Oddly, this advice is usually given by people who also warn us to avoid hubris in the Middle East. We can continue to urge Israel to halt the settlements, and to urge the Palestinians to reform their government. But we should not encourage the illusion that we can solve this conflict.

Finally, there is the vexed question of our relations with Europe— or rather, with European nations. Here our policies should be guided neither by a petty desire for revenge against France and Germany nor by the felt diplomatic imperative to make nice. Our interest lies in strengthening the power of our friends in Europe and marginalizing our foes. That means that we should continue to cultivate our ties to Eastern Europe. It also means that we should stop encouraging the centralization of political power on the Continent. For several years, we have told Eastern Europe to join the European Union and have blessed the EU's efforts to devise a common defense and foreign policy. It is hard to imagine a European policy more perversely counter to our interests. And it is time for the Bush administration to show the same boldness and imagination in its approach to alliance diplomacy that it has shown, to such good effect, in Iraq.

Bush's Illegitimate War

By David Corn

David Corn, editor of the Washington, D.C., office of the Nation, *a liberal periodical, argues in the following selection that U.S. president George W. Bush and his team were dishonest about their reasons for pursuing a military assault on Iraq. Before the war, for example, Bush said that Iraq was a serious threat because Saddam Hussein possessed weapons of mass destruction that he could provide to terrorists. However, after the war, Corn says the United States adopted a "lackadaisical approach" to searching for weapons of mass destruction. No immediate plans were made to send in expert teams to search for weapons, U.S. forces did not bothered to secure Iraq's most important nuclear site, and numerous other weapons of mass destruction sites remain unappraised. Concerning weapons of mass destruction, Bush's postwar actions belie his prewar assertions, demonstrating that he lied about the necessity of going to war against Iraq.*

More proof that Bush lied about the urgent need to wage war against Iraq is his failure to pursue democracy there after the war despite prewar claims that democratizing Iraq was a major reason for military action. Moreover, Bush hedged about how much the Iraq war would cost, according to Corn. Backers of the war will argue that the liberation of Iraq is worth the costs, but Corn calls it a swindle.

My fellow Americans, there may be threatening amounts of weapons of mass destruction in Iraq. There may not be. We're not sure. And if they are there, it may take weeks after military victory before we can launch a major effort to find and secure them. By then, they could be gone— that is, if they were there in the first place—perhaps in the hands of people who mean us harm. And after we defeat Iraq's brutal regime, the people of Iraq will welcome US troops as liberators. Then again, within days, many of them could be shouting, "Yankee, go home" and calling

for a new government dominated by fundamentalist religious leaders. We
don't know. Nor do we really know the extent of any operational links
between Saddam Hussein and [the terrorist group] Al Qaeda—if such
things exist. Still, I believe the potential risk posed by Saddam Hussein
is so great that we cannot let what we do not know to stand in the way
of decisive action. We cannot afford to guess wrong. With that in mind,
I have ordered . . .

With Baghdad conquered, the fog of prewar has started to clear.
And it now seems that had the Bush Administration been hon-
est with the American public (and the world), its on-to-war pro-
nouncements would have resembled the imaginary sequence above.
Instead, Bush and his national security team—including ex officio
members deployed in think tank bunkers and op-ed command centers—declared, without question or pause, that Iraq had dangerous
levels of weapons of mass destruction and that it was "urgent," as
[George W.] Bush said, to find and destroy these weapons. They also
talked about birthing a democratic government in Iraq without acknowledging obstacles and potential traps. But, it turns out, the Administration was not on the level. Moreover, it was woefully unready
to deal with the consequences of military victory.

Was Saddam Hussein Really a Threat?

Though Bush and other war cheerleaders had spoken of liberating
Iraq, their main argument concerned the threat posed by Saddam
Hussein. The reason he was such an immediate danger, they said,
was that he had these awful weapons and could, as Bush breathlessly
noted, slip them to anti-American terrorists at any moment. Yet once
US troops were in Iraq, the Bush Administration and the Pentagon
adopted a rather lackadaisical approach to locating and securing such
weapons. Weeks after the April 9 fall of Baghdad, the Pentagon was
still in the process of assembling a survey team of 1,000 experts to
search for chemical and biological weapons and signs of a nuclear
weapons program. Why had this force not been ready to roll at the
war's start?

During an April 17 press briefing, Defense Secretary Donald
Rumsfeld said, "I don't think we'll discover anything, myself. I think
what will happen is we'll discover people who will tell us where to
go find it. It is not like a treasure hunt, where you just run around
looking everywhere, hoping you find something. . . . The inspectors
didn't find anything, and I doubt that we will." Imagine if Rumsfeld
had said that before the war: We're invading another country to eliminate its weapons of mass destruction, but we won't find them unless

people there tell us where they are.

Bush had maintained that Saddam Hussein was a danger partly because he was close to possessing nuclear weapons. The US military, though, did not bother to visit Iraq's number-one nuclear site. A *Washington Post* story noted that before the war the vast Tuwaitha Nuclear Research Center held about 4,000 pounds of partially enriched uranium and more than ninety-four tons of natural uranium, as well as radioactive cesium, cobalt and strontium. This is stuff that would be valuable to people seeking to enrich uranium into weapons-grade material or merely interested in constructing a dirty bomb. Yet, the paper reported, "Defense officials acknowledge that the US government has no idea whether any of Tuwaitha's potentially deadly contents have been stolen, because it has not dispatched investigations to appraise the site. What it does know, according to officials at the Pentagon and US Central Command, is that the sprawling campus, 11 miles south of Baghdad, lay unguarded for days and that looters made their way inside."

Most of the facilities suspected of being used to manufacture or store chemical and biological weapons have also gone unexamined. On April 28 British Prime Minister Tony Blair said, "We started off, I think, with around about almost 150 sites [to search] and we were beginning to look at seven of them. Actually, the sites that we have got as the result of information now is closer to 1,000. . . . We have looked at many of those, but nothing like a majority of them." Days earlier, Judith Miller, a *New York Times* reporter embedded with one of four specialized military teams looking for WMD, noted (low in the story) that "two of the four mobile teams originally assigned to search for unconventional weapons have since been reassigned to investigate war crimes or sites unrelated to weapons." Sure, war crimes are important. But more so than finding weapons that can kill thousands and that happened to be the basis for the invasion and occupation?

Finding Weapons of Mass Destruction Not Enough

Toward the end of April, Administration officials, speaking off the record, were telling journalists it was possible none of these terrible weapons will be found. Nothing had even been located at the sites the Secretary of State cited in his crucial briefing to the UN Security Council in February. Only about 150 actual WMD-seekers were then even at work within Iraq—and some were complaining they were short on vehicles, radios and encryption systems. Gen. Tommy Franks, commander of allied forces in the Persian Gulf, said the search process would take months and probably involve "several thousand sites."

At any moment, US forces may find convincing evidence of chemical or biological weapons—which undoubtedly will stir rousing cheers of we-told-you-so from war backers. But that won't be enough. War was waged—so Bush and others said—to prevent Iraq's WMD from being transferred to people and groups who would use them against Americans. But the war plan included no schemes to prevent that from occurring. This was a dereliction of duty. Looters beat the United States to Iraq's nuclear facility. If Iraq had WMD, if Al Qaeda types were in Baghdad, and if these terrorists were seeking weapons of mass destruction in Iraq—the fundamental claims made by the Administration—then there is a good chance the nightmare scenario Bush & Co. exploited to win support for their war has already come true.

Why is Richard Perle not screaming about this from the roof of his French vacation house? Blair, for one, practically sounds bored with the topic of WMD. "Our first priority," he recently said, "has got to be to stabilize the country, the second is the humanitarian situation, and the third—and we can take our time about this and so we should—is to make sure that we investigate the weapons of mass destruction." Take our time? Wasn't the point that the United States and Britain could not wait one week longer before invading because it was necessary to neutralize the threat from these weapons?

So now they tell us. The Pentagon was not ready to go with an extensive WMD search-and-secure mission, and, after the war, there is no need to rush. And by the way, there might not be *any* WMD to show for all the effort.

Did the United States Really Plan for Democracy in Iraq?

The Administration was also unprepared—and disingenuous—regarding another purported aim of the war: bringing democracy to Iraq. In many cities, postwar dancing in the street quickly turned to stomping in the street, as Muslim clerics moved to gather political strength. But the rise of Shiite Power was not part of Bush's Iraq plan. Again, the *Washington Post:* "As Iraqi Shiite demands for a dominant role in Iraq's future mount, Bush administration officials say they underestimated the Shiites' organizational strength and are unprepared to prevent the rise of an anti-American, Islamic fundamentalist government in the country." But this was hardly an unforeseeable event. "Nobody who knows anything about Shiites and

Iraq are surprised by this," says Judith Kipper, director of the Middle East Forum. "There were people in the government who knew this. But they were on the desks, not in the room where decisions were made." Joseph Wilson, the last acting ambassador in Iraq, notes, "The Shiites always had aspirations. And the clerics have a constituency, an organization, a pulpit, an agenda, ambition and a trained militia. What else do you need?"

The Administration had a challenge for which it had not "wargamed." Did no one in the decision loop remember Algeria in 1991? That year a fundamentalist party that wanted to establish an Islamic state won national elections, and the military then waged a coup to prevent the party from assuming power. US officials have been saying the Iraqi people are free to plot their own government, yet Rumsfeld has declared that an Iran-style government is not an option. What if a majority of voters want something more Iran-like than USA-like?

Such knotty matters were not covered by Bush and his aides in their prewar speeches, which raised the rosy prospect of a domino effect spreading democracy from postwar Iraq to other states in the region. Nor did they address the difficulties of providing security to postwar Iraq. In fact, when Gen. Eric Shinseki, the Army Chief of Staff, testified in February that this could require 100,000 or more troops, Deputy Defense Secretary Paul Wolfowitz dismissed him as being "wildly off the mark."

But the war showed that the Administration and the Pentagon were not committed to effective postwar security. The national museum trashed, the widespread looting—Rumsfeld wouldn't even voice regrets about such events. These developments also were not predicted, even by the Pentagon, which decided to ignore such messy contingencies. "Months before the invasion of Iraq," the *Washington Post* reported in mid-April, "Pentagon war planners anticipated the fall of Saddam Hussein would usher in a period of chaos and lawlessness, but for military reasons, they chose to field a light, fleet invasion force that could not hope to quell such unrest when it emerged, Pentagon officials said." Was the public ever informed that US troops would rush to guard the oil ministry in Baghdad but not the three dozen hospitals in the city—even though Bush had promised in a prewar speech that "we will deliver medicine to the sick"? (He just didn't say when.) And one more dropped ball: As of late April, the Administration had not released a plan for overseeing Iraq's oil industry.

The Swindle of Americans

Another now-they-tell-us jolt has been the cost of the war. Before the invasion, Administration officials were fiercely tight-lipped, refusing even to hazard a guess in public (as if they couldn't even begin to estimate). In past weeks, the cost projections have ranged as high as $20 billion a year for a to-be-determined number of years. Despite Bush's prewar pledge of "a sustained commitment" to Iraq, some US officials talk of a sooner-rather-than-later pullout. Of course, that may conflict with the Administration's desire to have a friendly government in Baghdad. Occupations can be confusing. But weren't we informed of that? Actually, no.

Loose chemical and biological weapons. Nuclear material up for grabs. When-we-have-time WMD inspections. Those restive Shiites. Twenty billion bucks a year. None of this made it into Bush's prewar disclosure statement. War backers can—and will—argue that the outcome was worth the costs and the chaos. Indeed, the murderous Hussein is out; the Iraqi people are fortunately no longer at his mercy. Yet this was liberation by deceit and misrepresentation, and the scent of fraud hangs in the air. It's a swindle that, for the time being, benefited Iraqis but that undermined debate and democracy at home. And with projecting American power still a priority for Bush and his crew, a question lingers: What else are they not telling us?

The War's Unfinished Business

By Nancy Gibbs

*Reporter Nancy Gibbs argues that the American victory in Iraq is incom-
plete. Iraqis are free, but they are left with a shattered economy and uncertainty about the whereabouts of Saddam Hussein. Three key goals, the author says, must be met before the United States can claim victory.*

*First, U.S. troops must find Saddam Hussein and other high-level Baath
party leaders. Most Iraqis do not believe Hussein is dead, and as long as
he is alive, Iraqis will feel threatened. Second, the United States must find
and destroy weapons of mass destruction in Iraq. U.S. president George
W. Bush justified the war by claiming that Iraq's stock of chemical and biological weapons was a serious threat. U.S. officials believed that such
weapons would be easily found after the war ended, but instead have discovered that weapons caches have proved elusive. This situation raises
two possibilities, neither one good—either such weapons do not exist,
making the United States looks foolish, or they do exist but are not under
anyone's control. Third, the United States must create an interim authority
to run Iraq until elections can be held for a new government. Finding new
Iraqi leaders has proved difficult, however, as Iraq's various factions vie
for control.*

Nothing but a battle lost, said Wellington of Waterloo, can be half
so melancholy as a battle won. And so it is as the war in Iraq
turns into a fight for peace and a nation's soul. The conflict may be
over, but the combat hasn't stopped. Markets are open, but the lights
are still out, and there are shortages of everything but flies. Iraqis are
free to march through the streets demanding that U.S. troops pull out,
and to walk up to Marines and ask why there aren't more of them to
help keep the peace. The oil wells have been kept safe, but many ancient treasures are lost. Bodies have piled up, and the gravediggers

Nancy Gibbs, "Unfinished Business: America's War with Iraq Won't Be Complete Until U.S.
Forces Can Resolve Three Key Questions," *Time*, vol. 161, April 28, 2003, p. 40. Copyright © 2003
by Time, Inc. Reproduced by permission.

have disappeared, so it's up to people to bury their own. Peace is painted in more subtle colors than the black, white and blood-red days of war.

The looting has subsided, partly because there is nothing left to take. U.S. troops who began . . . as soldiers ended it as cops, trying to distinguish the bad from the worse. They did foil a bank robbery, recovering $3.68 million in American hundred-dollar bills from the thieves' car. But the ransacking of Iraq's national museum, home to some of the world's most precious antiquities, left a wound in the country's heart. General Tommy Franks took his victory lap through Baghdad, passing out cigars to his commanders and brushing off a legion of armchair generals who had cast doubt on his plan. Seven rescued prisoners of war were on their way home. Iraqis exchanged their dinars for dollars, 2,000 Saddams for one George Washington. For the first time in a generation, leaders from different regions and faiths and tribes met to imagine their future, and emerged with a 13-point platform.

The fact that both Saddam and his weapons were still missing made for some uncomfortable conversations in Washington—particularly when Saddam popped up again on TV. Virtually an entire air wing of Soviet-made MiG-25 fighters was found hidden in the desert, and more gold-plated AK-47s turned up in Saddam's palaces. But there was no sign yet of the buried nerve gas or a proven biowarfare lab. Polls in America are reflecting relief that the worst is over, more than concern at what remains to be done. But failure to achieve all the ends for which the war was launched may exact a higher cost over time.

At every briefing for weeks, U.S. officials have been asked how we would know when the war was over. Now CNN has changed its running headline to THE NEW IRAQ. A&E has a special called Saving Private Lynch. More than a dozen companies are looking to trademark the term shock and awe. "Victory in Iraq is certain," President George W. Bush said last week in the Rose Garden, "but it is not complete."

Leave it to Iraq's tenacious ruler to taunt his enemies and torture his people when he's supposed to be good and dead. Even after the second U.S. strike on a purported hiding place, even after his government had vanished and the statues had toppled, it required a leap of faith for the people of Iraq to believe he would never be able to touch them again. The streets of Baghdad itched with rumors. The Americans missed him by 10 minutes or 10 yards. He's in Russia, in Syria, on an island off the coast of Spain. No, he's right beneath our feet—he and a thousand guards hiding under the city in bunkers with a two-year stock of food and water, waiting to stage a coup when the

U.S. withdraws. No, he left last fall and went to North Korea, which offered shelter in return for help with its nuclear program. No, Saddam and son Uday were shot by younger son Qusay, who fled to Syria and is secretly negotiating a swap with the U.S.: clemency in return for Dad's dead body.

Among the vividest and most recurrent were rumors that on April 9, the day U.S. tanks rolled into Baghdad, Saddam appeared outside the Adhamiya mosque in the northern part of the city, rising from the sunroof of his limo to greet an adoring crowd, with Qusay at his side. So it was uncanny when something like that very scene played on Abu Dhabi TV late last week. The network said its source insists the video was made on April 9, two days after Washington launched a bomb strike that many suspected had killed Saddam.

The White House can argue all it wants that Saddam's fate does not matter strategically. But it matters psychologically. For Iraqis, the new sighting confirmed their belief that, as a Baghdad resident put it, "we must see Saddam's body hanging from a lamppost before we can be truly at peace" Every fire fight, every explosion, every low-flying jet supports the widespread conviction. "No one believes Saddam is gone," says Ramzi, a Kirkuk oil worker. As cabdriver Faras Ahmad explains, "we have all been trying to forget him, but he's telling us, 'I am still here.' If he is alive, then Iraq is not safe."

It will be days or weeks before U.S. intelligence analysts can confidently judge when the latest tape [purportedly made by Saddam] was recorded and what it means. At a glance, some officials doubted that a man who kept his own Republican Guards out of Baghdad for fear of mutiny would do a walkabout on the day his capital was stormed by a foreign invader. They suggested that the tape must have been made weeks earlier. But there had been clues for days that perhaps Saddam had escaped again. The U.S. had not yet sent a team to dig for proof—for his body or at least his DNA—at the site of the April 7 bombing. (Despite denials from Washington, officials at U.S. Central Command stuck by their claim that they have his DNA. Franks won't say how the sample was obtained, but sources point to a dental lab found at one of Saddam's palaces.) Pentagon officials now think that Saddam may have been hiding in a white-stuccoed house adjacent to the building that was destroyed: neighbors note that the house boasted five telephone lines and a wooden desk like the one Saddam sat behind during his television appearances early in the war. As many as 10,000 U.S. special-operations troops in the region are exploring palaces, tunnels, bunkers and other places where Saddam may be hiding—or where evidence may be found to help track him.

In the meantime, the Americans can take some satisfaction from a few big catches: after passing out the 55 playing cards depicting their most wanted, they began to take some tricks—two half brothers, the Finance Minister, a senior party official. Top science adviser Amir al-Saadi had surrendered the week before, and Imad Hussayn al-Ani, who is supposed to have been in charge of Saddam's VX nerve-gas program, turned himself in on Friday [April 25, 2003]. For good measure, Abu Abbas, mastermind of the Achille Lauro hijacking in 1985, was captured in Baghdad.

Where Are the Weapons?

Saddam was not the only thing missing. For months before the war began, everyone from [George W.] Bush on down argued that Saddam's arsenal of biological and chemical weapons was so dangerous that destroying it was worth a war. They laid claim to information so certain that [Secretary of State] Colin Powell was able to provide graphic details to a U.N. audience. . . . Pentagon officials were confident that the quality of their intelligence would lead troops to the illicit stockpiles fairly quickly once US. boots were on Iraqi soil. Now they're adjusting the picture: the Pentagon says its soldiers are no more likely to stumble over a weapons cache than top U.N. weapons inspector Hans Blix was. "Things were mobile. Things were underground. Things were in tunnels. Things were hidden. Things were dispersed. Now, are we going to find that? No, it's a big country," Defense Secretary Donald Rumsfeld said last week [April 21, 2003]. "The inspectors didn't find anything, and I doubt that we will—what we will do is find the people who will tell us."

However sanguine officials sound in public, in private the pressure is rising. The Pentagon dispatched an entire brigade—3,000 troops—to the search and offered $200,000 bounties for any weapons of mass destruction (WMD) uncovered. Local officers were authorized to make payments of $2,500 on the spot. "The White House is screaming, 'Find me some WMD,'" says a State Department official, adding that the task is one of many suddenly facing the department. Members of the Administration must feel a new bond with Blix, since they are now the ones arguing that these things take time.

Even the hard-liners concede that they have confirmed absolutely nothing so far. Soldiers rooting around with rifles and test kits stumble on something suspicious, and it's an instant headline. But barrels of nerve agent have turned out to be pesticide; tip-offs about weapons sites have gone nowhere; the buried or mobile bioweapons labs have so far failed to surface. A senior Pentagon official says U.S. forces have been to several "promising" sites in southern Iraq and have come up empty. "It's there, but it's well hidden," a second Defense official insists. "It will take time to discover and verify because they took time—and effort—to hide it." Some officials now question whether huge stockpiles will ever be found: it's easy to hide a liter of anthrax, but not the factory-size facility needed to produce it.

The failure to turn up anything to date raises two possibilities, neither one good, says Joseph Cirincione, chief of the Non-Proliferation Project at the Carnegie Endowment for International Peace in Washington. "It may be that there aren't as many weapons as the President said, in which case we have a major intelligence failure, a huge embarrassment for the President and a huge blow to U.S. credibility—and that's the good news," he says. "The other option is that there are as many weapons as the President feared, and they're no longer under anyone's control."

That second possibility underscores the urgency of the hunt. The prime rationale for the war was to prevent the proliferation of such weapons. Since every other government facility has been pillaged, there's no reason to believe such marketable weapons are secure. "It's not that no one knows where they are," Cirincione says. "It's that we don't know where they are." Iraqi detainees like al-Saadi and al-Ani are not likely to talk for fear of being prosecuted for war crimes. Both have been saying, as an intelligence official put it, "Weapons of mass destruction? What weapons of mass destruction? We have no stinking weapons for you." But everyone else, down to the janitors, is expected to cooperate once fear of reprisal is removed.

Then there is the political problem. The longer the hunt takes, the Pentagon concedes, the more likely it is that skeptics will charge that whatever is eventually found was planted by the U.S. In an interview with Der Spiegel, Blix said the information the U.S. provided to his teams before the war was "pathetic." So it was not surprising when he said . . ., "I think that at some stage they would like to have some credible international verification of what they find," suggesting that if the U.S. ever does uncover something, it will have to call for inspections on itself.

Who Is in Charge?

At sunset last Monday [April 21, 2003], Jay Garner climbed to the top of the 4,000-year-old ziggurat in Ur in southern Iraq and looked down over the remains of the city of Abraham's birth. The former three-star general, assigned to invent a democracy from scratch, was preparing to preside the next morning over the first freely convened meeting of Iraqi leaders in memory. "There we were, at the birthplace of civilization, and we were about to create a democracy," says Garner. "I had tears in my eyes."

That's about as moist and mystical as it gets from Garner. For all the lofty dreams of planting liberty in fresh soil, the Bush Administration dispatched a pragmatist with a low-key manner and rolled-up sleeves to get the job done. "Jay's way," as his subordinates call it, involves no waffling, full accountability, foot on the gas, getting results. He has a staff of 200. . . . "There is the physical thing—roads and bridges—we can do that; I have enough money for that," Garner told *Time*. . . . "And then there is the government—that is harder. We are remaking human lives here."

Just getting started was harder than anyone expected. Many ministries were looted, and some workers were still afraid to go to work. As an incentive, Garner's operation will give each returning worker an emergency one-time payment of $20, equivalent to a month's pay. As for order, some police officers went back to work in Baghdad, but all was not quiet there or in other cities. Those police officers were all products of the old regime, and many Iraqis were reluctant to accept them as arbiters of the new. In Kirkuk, says Ahmad Shakir, an Arab teacher from the Qadissiya district, Kurdish children with rocket-propelled grenades were going from house to house in his neighborhood, telling Arabs to move out in two days or die. "I went to the Americans to ask for help," he says. "They said it was not their responsibility; go to the civilian administration. I came to the local Kurdish authorities, and they tell me, 'Go ask the American soldiers.'"

As for finding a new generation of leaders, "It is like walking in a dark room holding your hands out, feeling for the walls and trying not to touch the furniture," says Garner. Discerning who is credible and who is corrupt requires trial and error. The night before the conclave [a meeting on April 28, 2003, of Iraqis to discuss Iraq's future], Garner met with exile leader Ahmad Chalabi of the Iraqi National Congress. He would not be attending in the morning—in many quarters there is deep opposition to him as a Pentagon puppet—but Garner wanted a chance to hear Chalabi's take on the situation. Pressed and proper in a tie and herringbone jacket, despite more than a week of living in a crumbling warehouse, Chalabi told the American proconsul the looting must be stopped so that citizens would feel safe. "We do not want Iraqis turning to Americans to solve their problems," Chalabi said. He wants Iraqis going to other Iraqis for help. But he didn't talk of how an Iraqi Interim Authority would be run or of his own future role, if any.

The 80 leaders who met the next morning represented just a first round: about one-third were Iraqi exiles; the rest were drawn from inside the country. "At the beginning there was a sense of a standoff between the outsiders and the insiders, but as the day wore on, you saw them sitting down with each other at the tables. I thought that was a good thing," says Garner. One Shi'ite cleric stood up and quoted Abraham Lincoln, much to Garner's delight.

But outside the tent, people weren't exactly celebrating. Thousands gathered to denounce the process or demand to know why they had been excluded. After Friday prayers, protesters swarmed the streets of Baghdad calling for Muslim unity. When a U.S. Marine patrol wandered around a corner into a Baghdad street filled with worshippers spilling out of a Sunni mosque, the flashes of anger and the wrestling for power captured in a second the challenge that American forces face. WE REJECT FOREIGN CONTROL, read the banners. The sheik's sermon was a hymn to nationalism: Do not try to divide Sunni from Shi'ite, he said; we are all united in our desire to create an Islamic state free of both Saddam and America.

At the sight of the U.S. forces, worshippers rose and formed a wall to block them. The Marines did not understand Arabic, but they did not need to: the angry shouting made it clear that they were not welcome. A staff sergeant tried to calm the crowd, telling demonstrators, who did not speak English, that his troops meant no harm. He finally lost his temper when an Iraqi said, "You must go." "I have the weapons," the sergeant replied. "You back off."

One stone tossed, one shot fired could have led to disaster. But the Marines retreated cautiously around the corner as the faithful were held back by their own men. Women peered at the soldiers from behind cracked-open doors, and children waved to them and gave them a thumbs-up as both sides edged back, for now. This is a new moment, a new mission, for the Iraqi people and for the soldiers in their midst, and the challenge for both is likely to grow as the future takes root.

CHAPTER 3

Challenges for Postwar Iraq and the World

Getting Iraq's Oil Flowing

By the *Economist*

In the following selection, the Economist *analyzes the problems associated with repairing Iraq's oil industry. Iraq has the second-largest oil reserves in the world, second only to Saudi Arabia. Both the United States and Britain promised both before and after the war that they did not seek control over Iraq's oil, acknowledging that it belongs to the Iraqi people. But getting Iraq's oil flowing raises many difficult questions. For example, it is hard to decide who will manage the oil industry in postwar Iraq—the United States, the United Nations, or the Iraqi Oil Company. It is also difficult to decide what countries will be permitted to sign oil contracts with Iraq or determine whether to honor oil contracts between Saddam Hussein and other nations, such as Russia and China. Also, a decision will have to be made on whether Iraqi oil fields will be controlled by the government or private businesses.*

According to the Economist, *the speed with which U.S. troops moved to protect the oil fields during the war caused speculation that U.S. control of the oil was a high priority for President George W. Bush and his administration. Moreover, rumors circulated that the United States might flood the market with Iraqi oil to lower oil prices for U.S. consumers. This, however, would be impossible because Iraq's oil industry is in severe disrepair, and it will take billions of dollars and at least a year to boost production to prewar levels. The difficulty of sorting out the many complex issues associated with rebuilding Iraq's oil industry is overwhelming, even for an established government. In Iraq's case, these problems must be addressed by an uncertain, interim government that will likely face questions and distrust no matter what decisions are made.*

W hat should be done to ensure that Iraq's oil is managed truly in the interests of its newly liberated people?

"If an oil tender is made by a legitimate government that can guarantee terms and conditions for the long term, we would certainly be interested." Those unusually candid words, uttered . . . by David O'Reilly, the boss of Chevron Texaco (an oil giant on whose board Condoleezza Rice, America's national security adviser, once served), seemed to confirm what conspiracy theorists have suspected: Big Oil cannot wait to get its hands on Iraq's oil reserves, said to be the world's second-biggest after Saudi Arabia's.

Already, the industry is abuzz over who will manage Iraqi oil in the short term: the United States, the United Nations or the Iraqi national oil company? There is lots of speculation too about opportunities for foreign firms, especially those from countries that participated in the fighting to oust Saddam Hussein. There are even suggestions—especially by free-market think-tanks, such as the Heritage Foundation—that Iraq's oil sector will be quickly privatised, at American insistence. Firms that hold contracts signed by the erstwhile dictator are getting nervous: Russia's Lukoil, which signed a deal to develop the giant West Qurna oilfield in 1997, . . . vowed to fight any attempts to overturn its contracts—by impounding Iraqi tankers if necessary.

Pitfalls for the United States and Britain

Yet America and Britain both made unequivocal promises long before war started that Iraq's oil belongs only to the Iraqi people, and that taking it played absolutely no part in the decision to go to war. In a joint statement on April 8th, George [W.] Bush and Tony Blair again made clear that Iraq's oil and other natural resources are "the patrimony of the people of Iraq, which should be used only for their benefit."

The trouble is, deciding what is the best way to manage Iraq's oil in the interests of its people is far from straightforward—and some of the most promising options may involve creating profitable opportunities for foreign firms, including American and British oil companies, which would be bound to play badly with those disinclined to take Messrs Bush and Blair at their word. Cynics even questioned the speed with which the coalition acted (with some advice from Big Oil) to prevent the destruction of Iraq's oilfields. Action that protected the Iraqis' patrimony was portrayed as fighting a war according to the priorities of the oil industry.

One conspiratorial forecast, at least, seems certain not to come true—which might quieten down the cynics sufficiently to let a proper debate ensue. It had been suggested that, having seized Iraq's oil, America would flood the market, lowering prices and destroying the bete noire of America's gas guzzlers, the OPEC [Organization of the Petroleum Exporting Countries] cartel. Most oil-industry experts reckon that this would manifestly not be in the interests of the Iraqi people. But it is equally clear that this could not be done in any case—at least, not within the sort of time period in which it seems likely that Iraq will be governed by some external authority, be it the victorious military coalition or the UN.

Misrule and under-investment, combined with a decade of UN sanctions that restricted imports of spare parts, have left Iraq's oil industry in tatters. It would cost billions of dollars and take the best part of a year simply to return to pre-war export levels of 2.5m barrels per day (bpd). To reach 3.5m bpd, last seen nearly three decades ago, would take another $5 billion–7 billion and several years, reckons Cambridge Energy Research Associates.

Complex Issues in Rebuilding Iraq's Oil Industry

As the comments by Chevron Texaco's Mr O'Reilly made clear, much will depend on how soon a legitimate government can be established in Iraq. But things would be tricky even if a democratic Iraqi government were ready to take office at once.

Such a government would have to find new people with industry expertise to run the Iraqi national oil company, replacing Saddam Hussein's cronies who were previously in charge. Billions of dollars are needed to repair damaged oil-industry infrastructure and raise output. There would be decisions to take about what role to allow foreign oil firms, and at what price—and whether to cancel contracts signed with foreign firms by the old regime. There would probably also be a debate about the proper relationship between the new government and the oil industry, including about the possible role and form of privatisation. Given the likely constraints on output for the foreseeable future and the pressing need to raise cash to rebuild the country, there would be tough decisions to take about whether to borrow using oil reserves as collateral, or even to sell them, either by securitising likely future revenues or direct to foreign oil firms.

That these issues will be even more complicated for any interim government is highlighted by the issue of whom to put in charge of the Iraqi national oil company, given that most experienced Iraqi oilmen are probably now unsuitable, if alive. It is easy to see why names such as Philip Carroll, a former boss of Royal Dutch/Shell's American subsidiary, are doing the rounds in Washington, DC—and equally easy to see why this generates cynicism.

Capital Needs

As for raising money, private-sector oil firms frequently borrow by pledging their reserves as collateral. Some countries, including Mexico, have securitised expected revenue streams from their state-run oil firms. But Amy Jaffe, an energy expert at Rice University, Houston, reckons that in Iraq, depending on who pays for what, the sums involved may dwarf those that other borrowers have been able to raise from the capital markets: "The costs of occupation and reconstruction will be $100 billion to $200 billion, and the Bush administration couldn't get even Goldman Sachs to do a deal that size!"

An alternative may be to persuade foreign oil firms to put up capital in exchange for the right to oil reserves, either through production-sharing agreements or full ownership. In such circumstances, the highest prices are likely to be obtained by having an auction open to all. Alas, any restriction of bidders to, say, firms from countries that supported the war, would clearly not be in the interests of the Iraqi people. Equally, contracts signed under Saddam were not in the best interests of the Iraqi people, both because firms from countries that abided by UN sanctions could not bid and because the deals were driven by Saddam's private interests. There are strong grounds for voiding those contracts and starting the bidding again.

Would that be legal? Some analysts argue it would be, given that Saddam Hussein was a dictator and that some of the contracts held by Russian, Chinese and Indian firms appear to have been granted to curry political favour at the UN and perhaps stave off an invasion. Other experts insist that any such move would represent a clear violation of property rights akin to Fidel Castro's expropriation of American assets four decades ago.

Vahan Zanoyan of PFC Energy, a consultancy, offers a real-world counterpoint. "In the oil business, sovereign governments can and sometimes do renege on oil contracts, which are always ultimately based on trust." Russian or Chinese firms could perhaps challenge Iraq or an American interim authority at the international civil court at The Hague, but that would merely guarantee that the companies would not see any oil or money for many years and probably never be able to work in Iraq again. He thinks that firms such as Russia's Lukoil, despite its current sabre-rattling, may ultimately decide to negotiate a settlement with a new regime, in order to salvage some value from their contracts, or perhaps sell their rights to American or British rivals.

Trusting the Interim Iraqi Government

Any decision by an interim government to sell Iraq's oil reserves, particularly as it would probably be to foreigners, would be hugely controversial and vulnerable to accusations of bad faith. If some other way of raising cash for rebuilding could be found—an IMF [International Monetary Fund]/World Bank loan with oil reserves as collateral, perhaps—that would surely be better. But there is one reason to fear leaving the ownership of the oil reserves to a new Iraqi government—namely, that its members would face an enormous temptation to expropriate them for their own advantage. There are strikingly few examples of countries that, having become wealthy thanks to their oil resources, share this wealth broadly across the population.

What to do to prevent this, and to what extent any interim government should try to persuade a new Iraqi government to pursue a particular course of action, or even present it with a done deal, is sure to provoke a lively debate.

Some reformers are likely to view Iraq as another opportunity to try mass privatisation, with shares in Iraqi oil given to every Iraqi. Perhaps they can improve on the failure of past mass privatisations, notably in Russia, when recipients of shares tended to sell them quickly at well below their true value. Others familiar with the failure of mass privatisations such as Russia's will argue that Iraq should avoid it at all costs, pointing instead to the likes of Norway, Colombia and Alaska, which created funds that hold oil revenues in trust for the people. In Alaska, for example, the state oil fund disburses roughly $8,000 each year to every family. Similar payouts would certainly provide Iraqis with hard proof that the oil is now theirs, not America's, not their new government's—and certainly not Saddam's.

Establishing an Interim Government in Iraq

By Mark Sedra

The selection below is a policy paper written by political analyst Mark Sedra, which was published by Foreign Policy in Focus *(FPIF), a joint project of the Interhemispheric Resource Center (IRC) and the Institute for Policy Studies (IPS), both public policy research groups. The paper addresses the issue of how to govern Iraq until a permanent government can be established. The author focuses on the possible models for an interim government.*

According to Sedra, the most likely model is an occupation government led by the U.S. military that will stay in Iraq for an indefinite period of time, perhaps with some multinational or UN assistance. This plan, which Sedra refers to as the neoconservative model, will likely require one hundred thousand to two hundred thousand U.S. troops to be stationed in Iraq for a five- to ten-year period. Under this scenario, the U.S. military would be responsible for governing postwar Iraq, distributing humanitarian aid, and overseeing Iraq's reconstruction. Reconstruction would be paid for by the United States, with help from countries that supported the war and from Iraqi oil revenues. Sedra concludes that while this plan offers the advantage of providing some security to fill the power vacuum left by the fall of Saddam Hussein's regime, this unilateral approach will likely create greater anti-American feeling in Iraq and neighboring Arab states, resulting in chaos in the Middle East.

A second model, which Sedra refers to as the Afghan model, would establish and interim government similar to the one set up in Afghanistan following the war against terror conducted there in 2002. In this scenario the United Nations would be responsible for establishing a democracy in Iraq

Mark Sedra, "Who Will Govern Iraq?" *Foreign Policy in Focus Policy Report*, April 2003. Copyright © 2002 by Interhemispheric Resource Center and the Institute for Policy Studies. Reproduced by permission.

and coordinating humanitarian aid following a ninety-day military occu-pation. Sedra maintains that this model has the advantage of avoiding the deepening of anti-American sentiments in the Middle East and would facil-itate humanitarian relief activities. Nonetheless, Sedra believes that the Bush administration will eschew this option and instead pursue the neo-conservative plan.

With Baghdad having fallen and the territorial consolidation of Iraq near at hand, discussion of the postwar period has inten-sified dramatically. The debate has provoked splits at various levels, within the United Nations, within the vaunted "coalition of the will-ing," and even within the U.S. government. The acrimony that has surrounded this debate shows that even with victory in the war as-sured, winning the peace will be a more arduous task. How Iraq is governed and rebuilt in the first two years following the war's con-clusion may determine whether, in the rhetoric of the Bush adminis-tration, it is transformed into a beacon of democracy for the Arab world or, as many Middle East experts and observers fear, it sparks a wave of violent and destabilizing unrest in the region. In light of the monumental significance of this enterprise, it is important to examine the potential models for postwar governance in Iraq and to assess their effectiveness and impact. An examination of public state-ments issued by policymakers who will shape the postwar dispensa-tion, along with an analysis of previous cases of post-conflict state building—such as post-World War II Germany and Japan, the Balkans in the 1990s, and, most recently, Afghanistan—provides a basis upon which to construct models of governance for Iraq. . . .

U.S. Neoconservative Model

The U.S. neoconservative model refers to the plan for postwar gov-ernment designed by the U.S. Department of Defense (DoD). It in-volves the establishment of a U.S. military occupation led by a high ranking U.S. military official, which will remain in place for an in-definite period. Lieutenant-General Jay Garner, a former army chief of staff and president of an arms company that provides crucial tech-nical support to U.S. missile systems, was handpicked by the DoD to serve as the occupation's military governor. Garner was appointed to lead the Office of Reconstruction and Humanitarian Assistance (ORHA), established in late January 2003 by a presidential directive to coordinate all U.S. planning for the post-war period in Iraq. This body gradually assumed the role of occupation government-in-waiting. The occupation government will consist of 23 ministries and three regional coordination offices, all headed by Americans. Each U.S. administrator will be provided with four Iraqi advisors, the majority of which will emanate from exile groups. In a concession to critics of the plan, Pentagon officials have indicated that some "soft ministries" such as health and education may be placed in the hands of Iraqis in the immediate aftermath of the war.

The main uncertainty regarding this plan regards the size and duration of the military occupation. DoD officials, such as Undersecretary of Defense Paul Wolfowitz, have emphatically rejected the notion offered by a number of defense experts and military figures, that a large force, consisting of more than 200,000 troops, would be required over a multi-year period to facilitate Iraq's political transition. In February 2003, Gen. Eric K. Shinseki, an influential military official, told the Senate Armed Services Committee that several hundred thousand U.S. troops would be needed to govern post-war Iraq. Wolfowitz later disparaged the assessment referring to it as "wildly off the mark."

The occupation force will likely be supplemented by an international stabilization force under the auspices of the U.S. occupation authority. The U.S. has already approached several pro-U.S. European countries about the possibility of contributing to such a force, including Denmark, Spain, Italy, Poland, Latvia, and Estonia. General Garner has supported Wolfowitz's contention concerning the size of the force and has indicated that the occupation will last no more than 4–5 months. Contrary to such optimistic appraisals, it will likely require 100,000–200,000 troops over a period of 5–10 years to achieve the stated U.S. objectives.

Under this framework the U.S. military would be responsible not only for governing postwar Iraq, but for distributing humanitarian aid and overseeing the country's reconstruction. The UN and international nongovernmental organizations (NGOs) would be largely relegated to an advisory role in the area of humanitarian relief. Similarly, prominent states such as Germany, France, Russia, and China would be, for the most part, frozen out of the reconstruction process.

The Pentagon would seek to pay for the occupation and rebuilding of Iraq with American tax dollars, aid from coalition powers, private sector investment, and Iraqi oil revenues. An American oil executive would be appointed to supervise Iraqi oil production, and the industry would be liberalized to allow U.S. companies to gain a dominant stake in it.

After order is established, authority would be incrementally transferred to an Iraqi interim government consisting primarily of Iraqi exile groups favored by the Pentagon. On April 15, 2003, the U.S.

military convened a meeting of Iraqi opposition groups in the southern city of Nasiriyah to select an Iraqi leader to work alongside the occupation regime. The meeting, which assembled internal and external opposition factions, resulted in a 13 point plan of action beginning with the imperative that "Iraq must be democratic." Perhaps more important than the results of the meeting was the conspicuous absence of the two main Shi'a opposition groups, the Supreme Council for Revolution in Iraq (SCIRI) and *Da'wa Islamiyah* or Islamic Call. The two groups, which enjoy considerable grassroots support among Shi'ites in Iraq, boycotted the event to protest U.S. domination over the process. The ire of these groups as well as many other Iraqi opposition leaders has also been provoked by the Pentagon's promotion of exile groups such as the Iraqi National Congress (INC). . . . The Pentagon has ferried members of the INC, including their controversial leader Ahmed Chalabi, into Iraq so they can solidify their position in the country. Although Chalabi did not attend the Nasiriyah conference he is being touted by many Pentagon officials as the leader of the interim Iraqi administration.

Advantages and Disadvantages of the Neoconservative Model

Although Donald Rumsfeld and his fellow neoconservatives at the Pentagon resolutely believe that this strategy can achieve the stated U.S. objective of creating a democratic Iraq and would spark a democratic domino effect in the region, the model's only advantage is that the massive U.S. military presence it entails would fill the security vacuum left by the fall of the Ba'ath regime. Unfortunately, even this advantage is negated by the violent backlash in Iraq that a U.S. military presence would undoubtedly provoke, a reaction that has already begun to materialize in cities across the country.

A number of factors make this model untenable. First, it ignores internal political dynamics in Iraq. The war has illustrated that although a large portion of the Iraqi populace may detest Saddam Hussein, the prospect of a U.S. military occupation is no more palatable. U.S. military and political leaders have continually underestimated the potency of Iraqi nationalism. Mounting civilian casualties coupled with longstanding mistrust of the U.S. due to its pro-Israeli posture have stirred anti-American sentiment, creating a dangerous atmosphere for an occupying force. . . . The jubilation of the Iraqi people immediately after the fall of Baghdad, marked by poignant images of Iraqis celebrating atop the ruined symbols of the Ba'athist regime, should not be misinterpreted as an endorsement of a continued U.S. presence. Once the reality of occupation sets in, the euphoric mood of the Iraqi people will likely shift to suspicion. The chants at a 150-person-strong demonstration protesting the U.S.-sponsored meeting of Iraqi opposition leaders in Nasiriyah, which included slogans such as "no to Saddam and no to America" and "no to occupation," clearly demonstrate growing Iraqi unease over the U.S. presence. . . .

The unwillingness of Shi'ite groups, who represent more than 60% of the population of Iraq, to cooperate with the U.S.-supported political process will obstruct the reconstruction process and complicate U.S. efforts to erect a legitimate transitional administration. According to A. William Saami, a Middle East expert for Radio Free Europe/Radio Liberty, "U.S. officials don't have a lot of traction in the Shi'ite community in Iraq . . . this is going to get worse before it gets better."

Most Iraqi exile leaders, even those closely associated with Washington, have summarily rejected the prospect of a long-term American military presence. At a recent conference of prominent Iraqi dissidents in London, a respected former Iraqi foreign minister, Adnan Pachachi, stated that "Iraqis will not accept foreign occupation of their country.". . .

Other Dangers of a Prolonged Occupation

The U.S. neoconservative plan fails to adequately take into account regional resistance to a U.S. occupation. Tension between the U.S. and the Arab world—already high due to America's support of Israel, the ongoing war on terror, and the Iraq war—will overflow if a long-term occupation of Iraq is instituted. An occupation will spark widespread resistance among the Iraqis and could conceivably stimulate an upsurge of support for terrorist activity throughout the region. Oil, in the eyes of many Arabs, will be the test that reveals Washington's true long-term intentions. As a former U.S. ambassador to Saudi Arabia has stated, oil "has become the symbol of colonial power, which all the countries of the region have experience with." U.S. efforts to aggressively assert control over the Iraqi oil industry would confirm the belief harbored by many Arabs that the U.S. has imperialist designs on the Middle East. If such a scenario unfolds, the apocalyptic warnings of Egyptian President [Hosni] Mubarak, that the U.S. war will produce "one hundred [Osama] bin Ladens," and that of Arab League Secretary-General Amr Moussa, that the war will open the "gates of hell," may yet come to pass.

The war, which has already killed thousands of Iraqi soldiers and civilians, has awakened and radicalized the Arab world. Joseph Cirincione, a senior associate at the Carnegie Endowment for International Peace, has astutely recognized that although the battle scenes beamed to the U.S. public by the likes of CNN make the war appear noble and heroic, "in the Arab world, it looks like a slaughter." According to Cirincione, "the American public does not understand the level of hatred growing in the Muslim world as a result of this war." This antipathy would only be amplified by an occupation, which could come to be viewed as an attack on Islam that must be universally resisted. Moscow's experience in Afghanistan, which resulted in the ignominious withdrawal of Soviet forces in 1989, illustrates the power of such perceptions to rally and unite the Arab and Muslim worlds.

The economic and material costs of any unilateral enterprise could also make it prohibitive in the long term. Reconstructing Iraq will likely cost up to $25 billion per year over a five-year span. Coupled with the cost of maintaining troops in the country, estimated by the Pentagon to be $2 billion a month, it is clear that this is a burden that Washington will be reluctant to incur without external support. Contrary to reassurances offered to beleaguered U.S. taxpayers, the Iraqi oil industry, whose infrastructure has been severely degraded by a decade of sanctions and war, will only cover a small portion of the costs of reconstruction. It is estimated that Iraqi oil will be capable of generating $14–16 billion per year in revenue after the war.

Complicating Iraq's economic situation, described by one economist as "a basket case," are its external debts and reparations. Iraq's external debt amounts to more than $100 billion and the compensation claims lodged against Baghdad from the 1990–91 Gulf War total more than $200 million. "Unless debt and reparations are dealt with properly, Iraq is basically bankrupt," according to Rubar Sandi, an Iraqi-American investment banker. The country will require an aid and debt relief program as ambitious as the Marshall Plan, if it is to overcome these economic obstacles.

UN or European Assistance Unlikely

Recognizing the dangers of a prolonged occupation, 52% of Americans have indicated that the UN should be in charge of governing a postwar Iraq, according to a poll conducted by the University of Maryland's Program on International Policy Attitudes (PIPA). However, with the military directing the humanitarian and reconstruction operation, there is little chance that the UN will be involved on a significant scale. Mark Malloch Brown, head of the UN Development

Program (UNDP), has made it clear that UN aid workers would not serve as subcontractors for the U.S. military. "It's not a mission where we can subordinate to military occupiers," Malloch Brown recently stated. He and other leaders of aid agencies have urged the U.S. to hand over the humanitarian operation to a UN coordinator. "To have the UN in charge would not only use its expertise to the fullest, but it would allow a broader multilateral coalition," said Kenneth Bacon, president of Refugees International.

In practice, the U.S. military has very little experience in delivering humanitarian aid on such a large scale. According to InterAction, a coalition of 160 U.S. humanitarian aid groups, it "would be the first time the American military has been in direct control of relief operations." The group has criticized the DoD's dominance of the reconstruction agenda, arguing that it "complicates (InterAction's) ability to help the Iraqi people and multiplies the dangers faced by relief workers in the field."

A multilateral approach that would share the costs associated with reconstruction would be very difficult to achieve under the neoconservative model. European governments, in particular, have openly declared their unwillingness to support a reconstruction agenda dictated by the United States. "A UN resolution will be a prerequisite for the full involvement of the EU in the postwar reconstruction (of Iraq)," Greek Foreign Minister George Papandreou told reporters after a meeting of European Union (EU) and North Atlantic Treaty Organization (NATO) ministers in Brussels. Arab states have joined the EU in advising against a U.S. occupation, and vital regional players such as Jordan, Saudi Arabia, Iran, and Egypt have ruled out any involvement in a U.S.-dominated reconstruction process. "Help the U.S. rebuild Iraq? No. Any attempt to impose a regime in Iraq is not seen as a welcome step in this part of the world right now," declared Nbil Osman, a spokesman for Egyptian President Hosni Mubarak. Expressing similar sentiments, Iranian president Mohammad Khatami has warned, that Tehran would "not recognize any administration other than an all Iraqi government." Regional and international support is essential to establishing a sustainable government in Iraq; without it, pursuing reconstruction would be like swimming against a strong current. . . .

Afghan Model

The second model that could emerge in postwar Iraq can be referred to as the Afghan model, because it would resemble in many respects the UN-led system implemented in post-Taliban Afghanistan. In March 2003, a UN task force under the leadership of Rafeeudin

Ahmed, a former UN Assistant Secretary-General recently appointed as special envoy of the United Nations secretary-general to Iraq, submitted a report to UN Deputy Secretary-General Louise Frechette outlining recommendations for UN action in postwar Iraq. The 60-page report was rooted in the premise that "the people of Iraq, rather than the international community, should determine national government structures, a legal framework, and governance arrangements."

Under the Afghan model, after a brief military occupation, perhaps lasting 90 days, a UN Assistance Mission, like the one established in Afghanistan, would be mandated by the UN Security Council to steer Iraq toward democracy and to coordinate humanitarian and relief activities. A UN approach has been widely endorsed internationally by members of the U.S.-led military coalition Britain and Australia, as well as by the EU, Russian, China, Japan, and the Arab League.

Along with the establishment of a UN Assistance Mission in Iraq (UNAMI), the UN would convene a conference to select an interim Iraqi government. Similar to the Bonn Conference held shortly after the fall of the Taliban, such a gathering would assemble important internal and external opposition figures and groups. The meeting would exclude all political figures perceived to have been tainted by the Saddam Hussein regime. UNAMI would assist the nascent Iraqi administration in governing the country and coordinating the work of UN agencies and NGOs, who would be responsible for the bulk of relief and recovery duties. Control over the Iraqi oil industry would be placed under the jurisdiction of the Iraqi interim government, with the UN and the U.S. jointly retaining an authoritative advisory role. After an interim period of up to two years, during which a Constitution would be drafted through an open and consensual process, UN-monitored elections would be held to choose a broadly democratic government.

The U.S. would retain a military presence, not exceeding 20,000 soldiers, during the interim period before democratic elections were held and a national army was rebuilt. The U.S. troops would be supplemented by a UN-mandated peacekeeping force similar to the International Security Assistance Force (ISAF) in Afghanistan. The primary U.S. role under this model would be to secure vital resources such as the oil fields, to avert the breakup of the country along ethnic lines, and to prevent regional states from interfering in Iraqi internal affairs. Like in Afghanistan, U.S. influence over the newly established government and the reconstruction process would be strong but integrated into a multilateral framework and orchestrated from behind the scenes.

Advantages and Disadvantages of the Afghan Model

The principal advantage of this model, in which the UN has a pronounced leadership role, is that it would confer a degree of legitimacy on the political transition and reconstruction process that would be lacking in the U.S. neoconservative approach. The humanitarian crisis would be more efficiently and effectively addressed under UN stewardship than if it were directed by the U.S. military, which has very little experience in managing large-scale relief operations. Also, awarding the mandate for reconstruction of postwar Iraq to the UN would be a major step toward healing the rifts between Europe and America and would ameliorate some of the damage done to the UN's credibility preceding the war.

The Afghan model also has several drawbacks. . . . In contrast to Afghanistan, which is largely rural, lacks significant natural resources, and has a population that is predominantly supportive of U.S. engagement—although this is rapidly changing—Iraq is a highly urbanized, resource-rich society with a distinctly anti-American disposition. Apart from questions of the suitability of the Afghan model in the Iraqi context, its effectiveness in addressing the needs of Afghanistan has been challenged by a recent upsurge of insecurity. The slow pace of development and security sector reform in Afghanistan currently threatens to undermine the Afghan reconstruction process, which is hardly an endorsement of this model for post-conflict Iraqi governance.

Another problem with the Afghan model concerns security. Since the Iraqi army was so intricately entwined with the Ba'ath Party apparatus, it must be totally dismantled and recreated in the postwar period. Thus, if the U.S. significantly scales down its military presence, a security vacuum will emerge. A large-scale peacekeeping operation will be needed to fill that security vacuum, even if the U.S. retains a force of up to 20,000 troops in Iraq. Under such conditions, UN, NGO, and military personnel would be dangerously exposed to any violent backlash that may occur. As in Afghanistan, a failure to adequately address insecurity can cripple reconstruction efforts. The lack of a strong military presence could also encourage one or more neighboring states such as Iran, Turkey, or Saudi Arabia to intervene in Iraq, raising the prospect of the country's Balkanization.

Perhaps the most profound problem besetting the Afghan model relates to the precedent it would set. If the UN is given the responsibility of leading the postwar reconstruction effort, it may be implied that states can defy international legal norms without repercussions.

By engaging in post-conflict reconstruction, the UN would, in effect, legitimize the U.S. decision to flout the authority of the Security Council, thus seriously eroding the UN's authority. . . .

Likely Model

There are strong indications that the U.S. neoconservative model, perhaps including elements of the Afghan model, will be implemented in postwar Iraq. It is unclear what impact the pleas of Tony Blair, [UN head] Kofi Annan and much of the international community in favor of a UN approach have had in Washington, but considering the Bush administration's current aversion to the UN, such pleas will have little effect. Although President Bush has promised that the UN will play "a vital role" in postwar Iraq, this will likely be limited to humanitarian relief and assistance, a position that the UN will find difficult to embrace in the context of a U.S. occupation.

Although [National Security Adviser] Condoleezza Rice has proclaimed that the U.S. "will leave Iraq completely in the hands of Iraqis as soon as possible," actions on the ground seem to contradict such rhetoric. The consequences of the neoconservative, unilateralist approach, if it is implemented, will be multifaceted and far-reaching. Winning the peace with such a strategy will be long and costly, maybe impossible. It will ignite unrest in Iraq and arouse the anti-American passions of the entire Muslim world, creating a fertile ground for terrorism. The long-term reverberations unleashed by such a policy will leave no nation in the region, and perhaps the world, untouched. . . .

The UN is best prepared to confront the massive humanitarian and political challenges that lie ahead for Iraq. This does not obviate the need for U.S. involvement; quite the contrary, U.S. engagement, on a political, economic, and military level, is vital for the success of this enterprise. Reconstructing Iraq will be a long and costly effort that would be difficult for any country, even a superpower, to accomplish alone. America's interests will not be served by transforming Iraq into a protectorate; this would only create instability in Iraq and exacerbate tensions along broader regional fault lines. If, as the Bush administration asserts, the primary goal of U.S. policy in postwar Iraq is to create a democratic system, then ceding authority over the reconstruction process to the UN would be the most effective approach to take. The televised conventional war may be over, but the question of whether hostilities will continue depends on the actions taken by the U.S. in the weeks and months ahead.

Democracy and Ethnic Divisions in Iraq

By Efraim Karsh

Efraim Karsh is head of Mediterranean studies at King's College, University of London, a visiting scholar at Harvard University, and coauthor of Saddam Hussein: A Political Biography. *In the following selection, Karsh argues that it will be difficult to establish democracy in Iraq given that Iraq has historically needed a strong, autocratic leader who could unite the nation, which has long been torn by ethnic strife. Religious and ethnic differences among Iraq's three main ethnic groups—the Sunnis, the Shiites, and the Kurds—continue to divide the nation.*

Karsh warns that creating democracy in Iraq will require that those ethnic differences be addressed. The most significant cause of conflict in Iraq, Karsh says, is the unjust distribution of power among the region's diverse ethnic and religious groups. For example, Shiites, which comprise the majority in Iraq, have been excluded from power and privileges by Sunnis. The Kurds in northern Iraq have not fared much better than the Shiites. A non-Arab ethnic group of Indo-European descent, the Kurds have fought a sustained fight against the Iraqi regime of Saddam Hussein and have sought to establish a separate Kurdish government. In 1988 Hussein instigated a massive campaign to completely eradicate the Kurdish population in Iraq, mercilessly destroying villages and slaughtering approximately five hundred thousand men, women, and children, often with the use of chemical weapons.

Karsh concludes that developing a democracy in Iraq will require a sustained effort by the United States. Pulling out of Iraq early, he claims, would constitute a betrayal of the Iraqi people and would most likely result in the rise of another tyrant as ruler of Iraq.

Efraim Karsh, "Making Iraq Safe for Democracy," *Commentary*, vol. 115, April 2003, p. 22. Copyright © 2003 by the American Jewish Committee. Reproduced by permission of the publisher and the author.

[A s] summarized in a late-February [2003] news story in the *New York Times*, "If [Saddam] does leave, the outcome may be messy, unpredictable, and very violent as old scores, suppressed by the governing Baath party for more than three decades, are settled." This messy outcome, moreover, has been said to pose an immovable obstacle to the dreams of a democratic Iraq with which the Bush administration has beguiled itself and the American people. "Could a democratic leader," the same *Times* report went on, "emerge in this deeply divided nation, which many Iraqis themselves believe requires a strong, even autocratic, leader to stay united?"

Saddam Hussein's Legacy of Violence

There is something to be said for this line of questioning. To it may be added the protracted legacy of political violence that has plagued Iraq since its inception as a state in 1921 and that, long before Saddam Hussein perfected his own spectacularly vicious system of enforcement, was the evidently accepted method of maintaining political order in that country. . . .

Saddam has undoubtedly been the most capable as well as the most savage player in this system. During his years in power—both as vice-president and de-facto leader after the return of the Baath to power in the late 1960's and as president since July 1979—he fully subjected the ruling party to his will, purging the country's governing institutions and reducing the national decision-making apparatus to one man surrounded by a docile flock of close associates. Preempting any and all dissent—Saddam's rise to the presidency was accompanied by the elimination of hundreds of party officials and military officers, including friends—he subordinated all domestic and foreign policies to the one and only goal of political survival.

Yet, like many tyrants before him, Saddam also gradually maneuvered himself into a position that required raising the stakes incessantly in order to survive. Each new acquisition of power engendered a greater fear of losing it. After three decades of external aggression and domestic repression, he has quite evidently failed to eradicate all potential dangers. Nor would some other dictator fare any better. Unless there is fundamental change in Iraq, there will be no solution to the predicament confronting the man at the top of the political pyramid. Whether Sunni or Shiite, Baathist or Islamist, military or civilian, he will continue to confront dissent and disaster at every turn.

The Promise of Democracy in Iraq

The status quo, in short, is no answer. But how realistic is the hope to transform Iraq into the first-ever Arab democracy? In an area of the world where the main instrument of political discourse is physical force, where the role of the absolute leader supersedes that of political institutions, and where citizenship is largely synonymous with submission, it can hardly be surprising that the Western ideal of liberal democracy should have been so glaringly lacking.

There are other complicating factors as well. Long after the fall of the Ottomans—the last great Muslim empire—the inextricable link among religion, politics, and society remains very much alive in the Muslim world, making the introduction of democratic ideals a daunting task. As we are constantly being told, there is no grassroots demand for democracy among Arabs and Muslims, and any attempt to impose it is bound to encounter stiff resistance and to arouse the proverbial "street" to new heights of anti-Americanism.

Nevertheless, and all these reservations notwithstanding, the September 11 [2001, terrorist attacks] have dramatically changed the West's overall calculus of cost and benefit, if only because they so starkly demonstrate the horrendous consequences of failing to address the Middle East's endemic malaise. Besides, it is not wholly inconceivable that, given the right guidance and support, Arab societies will indeed prove amenable to democracy; holding these societies to a lower political standard can be not only a recipe for inaction but a subtle form of racism. That is why the Bush administration's idea of "Iraq first," as a stepping-stone to a wider attempt to democratize significant parts of the Arab world, is of such far-reaching consequence and of such immense promise—provided, however, that the root causes for the lack of democracy in the Arab world are correctly identified and boldly addressed.

Britain's Exclusion of Shiites from Power

Any discussion of this subject must start with the fundamentally unjust distribution of power among the region's diverse ethnic and religious groups. Much has been written about the artificial nature of the state system in the modern Middle East. According to the received wisdom, the European powers (in particular France and Great Britain), having long set their sights on the territories of the declining Ottoman empire, exploited the latter's defeat in World War I to carve out a number of artificial states from its carcass. In so doing, however, they attended only to their own imperial interests, completely disregarding local yearnings for political unity. . . .

Britain was quite aware of the diversity and fragmentation of the Arabic-speaking communities of the Ottoman empire in general and of Mesopotamia in particular (as the region that was to become Iraq had long been called). As early as 1919, Arnold Talbot Wilson, the acting high commissioner in Mesopotamia, expressed deep misgivings about the country's fitness for immediate independence. Its predominantly tribal society, accounting for three-quarters of the population, lacked, he wrote, "previous tradition of obedience to any government except that of Constantinople," and possessed "an almost instinctive hostility to Arab 'effendis' in positions of authority." Wilson also doubted whether the almost two million Shiites would be prepared to acquiesce in the domination of their Sunni brethren, less than a third their number, and whether "the warlike Kurds in Mesopotamia, who number nearly half a million," would ever accept an Arab ruler. In sum, "far from making the Arabs on this side our friends," Wilson warned, "recognition of Faisal as king of Mesopotamia can only be regarded in this country as a betrayal of its interests, and we shall alienate the best elements here."

Yet by the spring of 1921 the British government had been sufficiently seduced by Faisal's London champions, notably T. E. Lawrence, to disregard these realities: to impose the foreign Sunni ruler Faisal (who hailed from the Hijaz, in today's Saudi Arabia) on a predominantly Shiite population, and to incorporate a large non-Arab Kurdish minority into the newly-created state. In so doing, the British effectively saw to it that the socio-political conditions that had existed during Ottoman times, when Shiites were excluded from power and persecuted by the authorities, would be perpetuated indefinitely.

Saddam Hussein's Repression of the Shiites

And so it proved. Over the ensuing decades, not only have the Shiites failed to play a role commensurate with their size in Iraq (where they constitute nearly two-thirds of the population), but they have also been ruled as an underprivileged class by the far smaller Sunni community (about a fifth of the population). Nor is this inequity in power the end of the story. In the 1970's, thanks to Saddam's ruthless development plans, the situation of the Shiites was made significantly worse as large numbers of them were compelled to migrate to the cities. In their miserable existence, they became fertile soil for anti-regime agitation, their resentment further fueled by their own religions authorities, the ulama, whose traditional position had been undermined by the Baath party's tight control over the state apparatus.

Religious animosities were thus piled on top of political ones. Organized Shiite opposition to Sunni rule had in fact begun to surface as early as the 1960's, in the form of an underground religious party, al-Da'wa al-Islamiyya, or the Islamic Call. Inspired by the teachings of the Ayatollah Muhammad Baqir al-Sadr, the Da'wa preached the replacement of the modern secular state by an Islamic order. Saddam, fearing the spread of religious fundamentalism, had taken steps to deal with this threat upon coming to power, and by the mid-1970's a number of Shiite ulama had been secretly executed.

But that hardly put a stop to the problem. In February 1977, demonstrations led by Shiite clergymen broke out in the holy towns of Karbala and Najaf, security forces were sent to restore order, and by the time the confrontation subsided, thousands of Shiites had been arrested and an unspecified number on both sides killed or wounded. Within a month, a special court was set up to try participants in the riots. Eight Mama were sentenced to death and fifteen to life imprisonment. The following year, the regime struck at the life-line of the ulama by taking control of all Shiite revenues.

Worse was to come in February 1979, following the overthrow of the shah of Iran and the rise to power in that country of a revolutionary Shiite regime headed by the Ayatollah Ruhollah Khomeini. Demonstrations in support of the new rulers of Iran in the Shiite areas of Iraq were met by military force, including tanks. Within months, martial law had been imposed and a repressive campaign was launched against the Da'wa and its leaders. In April 1980, Ayatollah Muhammad Baqir al-Sadr was executed together with his sister, and hundreds of Shiite political prisoners, most of them members of the Da'wa party, were placed before firing squads. Saddam sealed the southern part of Iraq, denying foreign worshippers access to Shiite shrines, and expelled some 100,000 Iraqi Shiites from the country.

The Kurdish Minority

In the Shiite experience in modern Iraq has been fearful, the country's other main ethnic group, the Kurds, have fared no better. A distinct group of Indo-European origin and of mainly Sunni faith, the Kurdish community, which comprises about 20 percent of Iraq's population, resides in the northern part of the country. In the wake of World War I, the Kurds were promised autonomy with an option for complete independence, only to discover three years later that they had been cheated: the Treaty of Lausanne between Turkey and the victorious Allies bore no specific reference to the Kurds, promising only tolerance for minorities in general.

Since then, the Kurds have been one of the largest aggrieved national minorities in the Middle East. The intractability of their situation stems from a geopolitical fact: they are dispersed across four

Middle Eastern countries—Iraq, Iran, Turkey, and Syria—each of which has had a vested interest in suppressing their national aspirations. This predicament has been further aggravated by the fragmentation of the Kurdish community along linguistic, clan, and tribal lines, a circumstance that has hindered the formation of a collective identity and facilitated the group's suppression.

Kurdish separatism raises the specter of the dissolution of the Iraqi state into three entities: Kurdish, Shiite, and Sunni. Had this happened early on, it might have rendered Iraq altogether nonviable, since approximately two-thirds of the country's oil production and reserves comes from the predominantly Kurdish areas, and the Kurds' fertile lands are Iraq's main granary.

But just as Baghdad has always been adamant about keeping Iraq whole, the Kurds, for their part, have conducted a sustained struggle against the central regime. . . .

Saddam Hussein's Persecution of the Kurds

In March 1970, Saddam, then vice president, signed an agreement with the foremost Kurdish leader, Mustafa Barzani, that contained far-reaching concessions to the Kurds. The most important was recognition as a distinct national entity deserving of autonomous rule; other clauses guaranteed cultural, linguistic, and administrative rights, the appointment of a Kurd as vice president of Iraq, and the enhancement of Kurdish representation within the state's ruling institutions.

But no sooner had the ink dried than Saddam reneged on his promises. According to the agreement, a census was to be held within four years to delineate the exact areas where Kurds constituted a majority. Mixed areas, in which no ethnic group formed a clear majority, were to be kept out of the proposed Kurdish autonomous region. This issue was particularly critical in the Kirkuk province, where Iraq's main oil fields lay and where the Kurds laid claim to a majority. Saddam, who did not for a moment contemplate Kurdish control over the country's economic heartland, launched an ethnic-cleansing operation: in September 1971, some 40,000 Kurds were expelled to Iran on the grounds that they were not really Iraqis, and in 1972 tens of thousands more were forced out.

Harsh as these measures were, they paled in comparison with the treatment meted out to the Kurds during the eight-year war between Iran and Iraq (1980–88). In early 1988, as the end of the war seemed in the offing, Saddam embarked on a massive punitive campaign aimed at the complete eradication of the Iraqi Kurds as a distinct socio-political community. Named the Anfal campaign, the operation reached heights of brutality exceptional even by Saddam's merciless standards. Like a steamroller crushing everything in its way, the Iraqi army advanced through the Kurdish regions, indiscriminately spreading death and destruction. Villages were shelled or bombed before being stormed by the army. Then the villagers were rounded up, with the women and children separated from the men and sent to "hamlets" elsewhere. The men and boys were often summarily executed or dispatched to concentration camps in the southwestern Iraqi desert, never to be heard from again.

By the time this horrendous campaign came to an end in the autumn of 1988, thousands of villages and towns in Kurdistan had been demolished and their populations deported. Some half-million Kurds had been ethnically cleansed, while another 250,000 had fled to Turkey and Iran. The international community became vaguely concerned with this genocidal campaign only because of the extensive Iraqi use of chemical weapons, including mustard gas, cyanide, and tabun nerve agent. The most appalling incident took place in March 1988, when Iraqi forces employed gas on an unprecedented scale against the town of Halabja: 5,000 Kurds—men, women, children, and babies—were killed on that day, and nearly 10,000 suffered injuries.

A Post-Saddam Iraq

This historical record casts a black shadow on the idea of Saddam as protector of Iraq's territorial integrity. Not only has he failed to cement the disparate components of Iraqi society into a unified whole, but he has significantly exacerbated domestic factionalism. . . .

Far from ensuring Iraq's survival as a nation-state, then, Saddam's continued rule poses the gravest threat to its very survival. By the same token, Saddam's removal from power could both liberate the Iraqi people from decades of brutal repression and safeguard the country's continued existence as a unified whole. Above all, it would create an opportunity, for the first time in nearly a century, to place the Iraqi state on a representative basis, one that truly reflected the "general will.". . .

Many people have devoted themselves to imagining what such a post-Saddam Iraq might look like. According to one detailed proposal, prepared . . . by a group of Iraqi exiles headed by the prominent intellectual Kanan Makiya, a "transitional authority" chosen by Iraq's opposition groups would start operating inside the country as soon as the regime began to crumble. After the fall of Saddam, the plan calls for the complete dismantling of the Baath party and the establishment of a war-crimes tribunal and a truth commission to oversee an Iraqi equivalent of the de-Nazification of Germany after World War II. The report envisions a state based on thoroughly secular principles, emphasizing protections for the rights of minorities. Most importantly, it sketches a new system of government—a modified federalism whose constituent parts would be defined along geographical rather than ethnic lines.

There is little doubt that Iraq's best hope lies with the creation of some sort of decentralized federal system in which each of the country's ethnic and religious groups would be given a proportional share in national power and resources, as well as extensive cultural and political autonomy in its main place of residence. The clear results would be to elevate the majority Shiites to a position of political preeminence at the expense of the Sunnis, and to integrate the Kurds into the country's governing structures. The transformation would not be limited to cosmetic changes at the top (such as through the appointment of a Shiite president, a Sunni prime minister, a Kurdish foreign minister, and the like), but would be extended across the entire spectrum of civilian and military life. . . .

In their report, Makiya and his fellow Iraqi exiles suggest that ethnic identity should be precluded as a basis for the new Iraqi state. As long as Iraq is defined as an Arab state, they argue, other ethnic groups, like Kurds and Assyrians, will continue to be second-class citizens.

This is a profound insight. Arab Iraqis must view themselves as Iraqis first, Arabs second; only thus can they avoid being torn by internal domestic schisms and implicated in imperial adventures. To generalize the same point beyond Iraq, one might say that only when the political elites of the Middle East reconcile themselves to the reality of state nationalism (wataniya) and forswear the imperial dream (qawmiyya) will the likes of Saddam Hussein be fully discredited. Similarly, only when the "pan-" factor has been banished from the Middle East's political vocabulary and replaced by a general acceptance of diversity will all the inhabitants of the region be enabled at last to look forward to a better future.

The Need for a Prolonged U.S. Commitment

And what role are the United States and its allies to play in this drama? As the Middle East faces its most defining period since the end of World War I, one cannot help being struck by the similarities between the present situation and that moment. The world has of course changed fundamentally since then. The age of imperialism is long gone, and by no stretch of the imagination can today's U.S. be compared with the former European empires in terms of self-perception, world outlook, or foreign-policy goals. . . .

Nearly a century later, the choices confronting the Bush administration are starkly reminiscent of those faced by Britain after World War I. Should the U.S. throw its full weight behind the implementation of its ambitious ideals, or pull out shortly after the overthrow of Saddam and the destruction of his deadly arsenal, most probably resigning itself to the substitution of another Iraqi strongman for the deposed tyrant?

Given Iraq's violent experience during the past half-century, this latter option would almost certainly amount to a betrayal of the Iraqi people. Just as the creation of free and democratic societies in Germany and Japan after World War II necessitated, above and beyond the overthrow of the ruling parties, a comprehensive purge of the existing political elites and the reeducation of the entire populace, so Iraq must undergo a profound structural reform if it is to know representative government. This is certain to be a difficult process, one requiring an extensive American military presence (and, no doubt, occasional military operations) over a protracted period of time, as well as a sustained commitment of financial, administrative, and political aid. But if history tells us anything, it is that any other alternative is an assured recipe for disaster.

The War in Iraq and the Demise of International Institutions

By Paul Johnson

In the following selection, historian and journalist Paul Johnson argues that the U.S./British war in Iraq is likely to be viewed as the first significant event of the twenty-first century. The reason that the war will be seen as significant is that it showed the need for change in international organizations such as the United Nations (UN) and the North Atlantic Treaty Organization (NATO). The UN, he claims, is hopelessly out of date. UN members commonly recognized as terrorist and rogue states have as much voting power as law-abiding nations. NATO, Johnson says, was created largely for the purpose of protecting Europe from Soviet expansionism and, since the Cold War ended, is obsolete. Johnson argues that the war in Iraq also served to highlight the weakness of the European Union, some of whose members disapproved of the war. Designed to bring European nations together, the EU has formed an economic union but has failed to develop a common foreign policy or armed force. With birth rates decreasing, it is unlikely that the EU will be able to finance a strong military, suggesting that the EU, like the UN and NATO, has no future.

Given the failure of these institutions, Johnson claims that Britain will probably join a group of English-speaking, democratic states with common traditions of law, language, culture, and morality. Led by the United States and including countries such as Canada, Australia, and New Zealand, this group will expand to include Asian countries and will be the main agent for maintaining a peaceful and law-abiding world.

Paul Johnson, "A World Shaken Up: Consequences of the First Important Event of the 21st Century—Good and Bad," *National Review*, vol. 55, April 21, 2003. Copyright © 2003 by National Review, Inc., 215 Lexington Avenue, New York, NY 10016. Reproduced by permission.

The Anglo-American action in Iraq, to which the Arab terrorist attack on September 11 [2001] was the prolegomenon, is likely to rank as the first important event of the 21st century. The reasons are twofold, the first negative, the second positive.

The UN and NATO Are Obsolete

The action, and responses to it, brought to the surface the need for fundamental change in various international organizations. The first is the United Nations, an omnium-gatherum of states whose permanent membership on the General Assembly and whose periodic membership on the Security Council is automatic without any regard to their qualifications. Thus military dictatorships, gangster-run states, and failed states overrun by terrorists have voting rights as valid as those exercised by law-abiding states that have succeeded in making democracy work and abided by the rule of law.

Moreover, the Security Council system, invented in 1945, is more than half a century out of date and no longer corresponds to global realities. These weaknesses explain why the U.N. failed even to address the problem of international terrorism, let alone deal with it. When, following 9/11, America, as the injured power, finally determined to do so, it found the U.N. an obstacle, not a help. The U.S. government suspected this all along, and involved the U.N. machinery only at the urgent request of its principal ally, Britain. In the event, the Allies refused the requests of France and Russia for bribes in return for allowing the U.N. machine to function. This rejection of the U.N.'s characteristically corrupt way of doing things amounted to rejecting the U.N. altogether. The U.N.'s failure to involve itself in the first major crisis of the 21st century effectively ends any attempt to make it an instrument of world government.

Second, the use made by the French government (and its temporary ally Germany) of the NATO structure to impede America's plans to act in Iraq again exposed the antiquity of an organization that had fulfilled its original purpose—to protect Western Europe from Soviet expansion—and showed conclusively that it is now obsolete. There is, indeed, no further point in keeping large forces from the U.S., U.K, and Canada in central Europe, and their withdrawal at this point becomes inevitable and urgent.

The question of what should replace these two organizations, both damaged beyond repair, is linked to a third negative event—the crisis inside the European Union. This was inevitable sooner or later, for the EU, in its fundamental structure, is also half a century out of date. It has proceeded systemically toward some forms of economic union, including a common currency, and is now contemplating a constitutional union. But it has made no progress at all toward a common foreign policy, and has actually gone backward from a common armed force to give it muscle, since the "European Army" proposal was voted down by the French in 1954. Britain excepted, the armed forces of the EU member states have declined in size and effectiveness in relation to the rest of the world, and there are no present proposals to modernize them. This helps to explain the EU's total failure to solve the biggest problem on its own doorstep, the disintegration of Yugoslavia in the 1990s. Indeed Continental Europe is physically and morally incapable of acting outside its own borders.

This weakness is likely to become more pronounced as the 21st century progresses. The four largest EU Continental powers now have some of the world's lowest birth rates: France, Spain, Germany, Italy (in descending order), and the portion of the total population dependent on the workforce is the highest in the world (Japan excepted). As the EU specifies a 35-hour working week, soon to be reduced to 30 hours, it will become increasingly difficult to finance existing pension commitments, let alone future ones dictated by demographic definitions. It is unrealistic to suppose EU governments will be willing or even able to support large armed forces.

A U.S.-led Coalition Will Be the Future

By contrast, the U.S., with a comparatively high birth rate, and with policies that enable it to absorb more high-quality immigration than the rest of the world put together, is poised to increase its demographic wealth base. Its population is now approaching the 300 million mark and is expected to pass 400 million by midcentury.

Seen against this background, criticism of Tony Blair for "positioning Britain too far from Europe and too close to America" seems singularly lacking in realism. In fact, Blair has been guided by his moral principles and by his accurate judgment of the relative integrity of America and Europe. But if he had been acting simply on principles of Realpolitik, the answer would have been the same.

Let us now look at the positive aspect. Without the means of defending itself, and with its power, wealth, and numbers declining every year, the EU has no long-term future, and it is becoming startlingly obvious, anyway, that Britain has no long-term future in it.

Events have obliged Britain to act with the U.S. in Iraq and that is likely to remain the pattern. With the marginalization of the U.N., the disintegration of NATO, and the enfeeblement of the EU, the future of Britain seems more likely to be secure as part of a constellation of democratic states with common traditions of law, language, culture, and morality, grouped around the U.S. and including other English-speaking peoples such as the Canadians, Australians, and New Zealanders. As English becomes even more a world language, the choice of participants will widen. An Atlantic free-trade union, including Britain, to which an Australasian and Pacific appendix (including, for instance, Singapore) would be added, seems the first, obvious step in this direction.

The U.S. will not allow its irritation with certain European states to influence its policy emotionally. Global policy must be determined by strict national interest. But this points increasingly to bringing the great Asian communities—India, China, and Japan—into America's plans for a peaceful and law-abiding world, for which a majestic combination of the English-speaking states will provide the democratic, military, and, indeed, moral leadership.

A Destabilized Postwar World

By Joseph Cirincione

Joseph Cirincione, director of the Nonproliferation Project of the Carnegie Endowment for International Peace, a private nonprofit organization focusing on international affairs, argues in the following selection that the consequences of the war in Iraq may be worse than the regime of Saddam Hussein and may not improve U.S. national security. Cirincione outlines four likely consequences of the war. First, he argues that the war may result in greater instability in the Middle East. Resistance to U.S. troops in the region is already growing and anti-American sentiments will likely increase. Second, Cirincione claims there may be an increase in terrorism as a result of the war. Indeed, hostility toward the United States as a result of the war can be used by terrorist leaders to recruit more terrorists. Third, Cirincione says the U.S. decision to strike Iraq without United Nations approval may weaken international alliances, leading to fears about U.S. hegemony. Finally, Cirincione suggests that, contrary to its stated goals, the war might actually increase nuclear proliferation. Rogue countries such as North Korea might speed up production of nuclear weapons to defend against U.S. military strikes. Conditions in the postwar world, Cirincione concludes, may provide less security to the United States and the rest of the world.

W e already have a fairly good idea of what the world will look like after the Iraq War is concluded and the Iraq Occupation begins. If President [George W.] Bush's vision of a quick military victory, a benign and untroubled occupation and the quick construction of a democratic Iraq is correct, then the rules and structures of the international system may be completely rewritten in favor of a U.S.-centric system.

However, the future is unlikely to be so obliging. The reason so many governments and experts urged Iraqi disarmament short of war is that the consequences of the invasion are likely to be mixed at best and possibly catastrophic. This concern does not underestimate the brutality of the Iraqi regime, but reflects a fear that the war cure is worse than the Saddam disease.

Here are four likely consequences of America's first pre-emptive war.

For administration hawks, Iraq is the beginning, not the end. Iraq is the start of a plan to change all the regimes in the Middle East. "There is tremendous potential to transform the region," says Richard Perle. "If a tyrant like Saddam (Hussein) can be brought down, others are going to begin to think and act to bring down the tyrants that are inflicting them." U. S. troops will be there to help in these transformations, operating from new, more secure bases in Iraq.

It is more likely that the mass movements in the war's wake will be anti-American, not pro-democracy. Arab citizens, already inflamed over what they consider the brutal military assaults of [Israeli president] Ariel Sharon's government and willing to excuse suicide bombers, will see American troops as Israeli reinforcements, not Iraq's liberators.

Fatwas are already flowing from mainstream clerics urging Muslims to resist the US. invasion. Governments may indeed fall, but it may be the rulers in Jordan that are threatened, not the dictatorship in Syria.

Terrorism Will Increase

For the president, terrorism is the new communism. "Freedom and fear are at war," he says "and we know that God is not neutral between them." There are no credible connections between Baghdad and [the terrorist group] al Qaeda, but in the president's mind the two are one and thus, he promised the nation, "The terrorist threat to America and the world will be diminished the moment that Saddam Hussein is disarmed."

But the war—whatever the outcome—will likely increase both amateur and organized terrorism. Much of the terrorism will be spontaneous outrage at the invasion and deaths, striking out at close by, identifiable American targets.

Some will certainly be sophisticated attacks on the American homeland. "An American invasion of Iraq is already being used as a recruitment tool by al-Qaeda and other groups," a senior American counterintelligence official told *The New York Times.* "And it is a very effective tool."

Never before has a U.S. president so scorned world opinion. [Harry] Truman had the United Nations with him in the Korean War, [John F.] Kennedy had the Organization of American States backing his blockade of Cuba; [Bill] Clinton had NATO in the war in Kosovo. Bush goes almost alone. The United Nations and NATO will never be the same. They and other multilateral institutions are now under pressure from both sides.

U.S. neoconservatives have already targeted the United Nations for destruction. "The United Nations is not a good idea badly implemented. It is a bad idea," says columnist George Will.

On the other side, there is deep distrust of Bush and his vision to transform the world the staid *Financial Times of London* opined, "The measure of this diplomatic fiasco is that a perfectly arguable case about one of the most despicable dictators of modern times was so mishandled that public opinion internationally came to worry more about the misuse of U.S. power than about Saddam Hussein."

Of the 200 countries in the world, U. S. claims 40 governments support the war. And the people of almost all these nations actually opposed the attack in overwhelming majorities.

If the war goes well, world publics may fear emboldened, postwar U.S. intentions even more. The Bush doctrine seems likely to generate exactly the anti-U.S. coalitions that it was designed to discourage.

What lesson will North Korean or Iranian leaders draw from the war? Will they curtail their nuclear ambitions, or speed them up?

If inspections had been given a chance to work, if Hussein had been disarmed without war, it would have been seen as a tremendous victory for Bush and as the world's enforcement of international treaties.

This is now Bush's War, a highly personal vendetta and exercise in raw power. Worse, to justify war, the Bush administration has disparaged inspections, thus undercutting future applications in Iran or North Korea.

But the impact may be more immediate.

If the war destabilizes Pakistan, nuclear weapons, materials or scientists may flow to other nations or terrorist groups. North Korea, ignored during the crisis, may go overtly nuclear, pushing nuclear ambitions in South Korea or even Japan. Iraqi military officers or scientists, fearing war crime trials, may flee invading U.S. troops carrying their knowledge or even weapons with them to other nations or groups.

The "bold stroke" so long sought by administration hawks has now hammered not only Hussein's regime but the international institutions so patiently constructed by Democrats and Republicans over the past 60 years. It will destabilize the region, increase terrorism, decrease alliance unity and make the spread of deadly weapons more likely without measurably increasing our national security.

That will be the postwar world.

⬢ CHRONOLOGY

3100 B.C.
The civilization of Sumer—characterized by developments in irrigation, trade, and writing—thrives.

1258 A.D.
Baghdad falls to the Mongols.

1533–1534
Iraq is conquered by the Ottoman Empire.

1914
After Turkey enters World War I on the side of the Germans, British forces invade southern Iraq.

1917
British occupation of Baghdad begins.

1920
Iraq, with its current boundaries, is created as a British colonial monarchy.

1932
Iraq becomes a sovereign state.

1958
Iraq becomes a republic when the monarchy is overthrown in a military coup led by General Abdul Karim Kassem.

1963
Kassem is overthrown by a group of officers, mainly from the Baath Party. Abdul Salam Arif becomes the new president.

1966
President Arif dies and is succeeded by his brother, Abdul Rahman Arif.

1968
Arif is overthrown, and the Baath Party seizes power in Iraq. Sad-

dam Hussein's cousin, Ahmad Hasan al Bakr, becomes president, and Hussein arises as a key leader in the party.

1974–1975
Kurds rebel, with the backing of the shah of Iran. Hussein is instrumental in suppressing a Kurdish rebellion by negotiating an end to Iranian support for the Kurds in exchange for which Iraq agrees to share sovereignty of the Shatt al Arab waterway, which provides access to the Persian Gulf.

1979
Hussein becomes president and immediately purges all opposition through terror. Ayatollah Khomeini comes to power in Iran as head of a revolutionary Islamic movement; Hussein feels threatened by Iran's encouragement of Shia uprising against Hussein's Sunni regime. Iraq attacks Iran, and the Iran-Iraq War begins.

1982
Israel bombs an Iraqi nuclear facility in a unilateral strike, destroying the reactor.

1984
UN investigators report that Iraq has used mustard gas and the nerve gas Tabun against Iranians in the Iran-Iraq War.

1987
The United States agrees to offer protection to Kuwaiti oil tankers in the Persian Gulf to prevent an attack by Iran. The United States is pulled into the Iran-Iraq War on the Iraqi side, thereafter providing military and surveillance assistance throughout the war. The United Nations passes Resolution 598 to end the Iran-Iraq War.

1988
The United Nations cease-fire goes into effect to end the Iran-Iraq War.

1989
Hussein uses chemical weapons against civilian Kurds in the town of Halabja, leaving five thousand dead and ten thousand wounded and destroying thousands of villages.

1990
Iraq threatens to use force against Arab oil producers who drive

prices down by exceeding their OPEC quotas. The next day, Iraq accuses Kuwait of stealing $2.4 billion worth of oil over the past decade from the disputed Rumaila oil field along the common border. Iraq also demands that Kuwait forgive an estimated $12 billion in loans given to Baghdad during the Iran-Iraq War.

August 2: Iraq invades Kuwait, and the UN Security Council unanimously passes Resolution 660, condemning the invasion and demanding Iraq's unconditional and immediate withdrawal.

August 6: The UN Security Council passes Resolution 661, imposing economic sanctions and authorizing nonmilitary measures to enforce trade sanctions.

November 29: The UN Security Council passes Resolution 678, authorizing member states to use force unless Iraq leaves Kuwait by January 15, 1991.

1991

January 16: U.S.-led coalition forces attack Iraq, and the Gulf War begins.

January 17: President George H.W. Bush addresses the nation, announcing the attack on Iraq and explaining the objectives of the war—to destroy the Iraqi military arsenal (including nuclear and chemical facilities) and liberate Kuwait.

February 28: The Gulf War ends.

March 2: The UN Security Council passes Resolution 686, demanding that Iraq cease all hostile and provocative actions by its forces against coalition members and implement all Security Council resolutions, including those requiring disarmament by Iraq.

April 4: The UN Security Council passes Resolution 687, creating the United Nations Special Committee on Iraq (UNSCOM) to monitor and verify Iraqi compliance with UN disarmament requirements and requiring the certified destruction of Iraq's weapons of mass destruction as a condition for ending economic sanctions. Later, a northern no-fly zone is created by the United States and its allies to protect northern Kurds from Saddam Hussein.

1992

The United States and its allies create a southern no-fly zone.

1993

After Iraq makes incursions in the southern no-fly zone and blocks inspection of weapons sites by UN inspectors, U.S., British, and

French forces conduct air strikes against Iraqi military sites, causing Iraq to back down.

1994

U.S. intelligence agents learn that Iraq has been deploying military divisions near the Iraq-Kuwait border. The United States sends troops to the area and warns Iraq; Iraq draws back its forces and accepts the Kuwait border.

1995

Hussein Kamel al-Majid, who headed Iraq's weapons of mass destruction program, defects, and the world learns that Iraq has a large biological weapons program and has weaponized some biological agents.

1996

Warfare erupts between two Kurdish factions in northern Iraq, an area under U.S. protection; Hussein sends troops, and the United States conducts missile strikes (Operation Desert Strike); Iraq pulls back its forces. The UN Security Council passes Resolution 986, authorizing an oil-for-food program to ease the humanitarian effects of sanctions, which allows Iraq to sell oil to buy humanitarian items.

1997

Hussein declares several weapons inspection sites to be "presidential" and therefore off-limits to UNSCOM.

October 31: Saddam Hussein announces his refusal to allow any further UN weapons inspections; at this time UNSCOM reports that it has made "significant progress" in disarming Iraq.

November: President Bill Clinton declares that sanctions should last until Hussein is removed, disagreeing with the Gulf War ceasefire provision stipulating that sanctions would be lifted when Iraq complied with UN weapons inspections.

1998

The United States warns Iraq of military strikes if defiance of the weapons inspections program continues; Iraq allows inspectors back into Iraq. The UN signs the Memorandum of Understanding with Iraq, agreeing to respect Iraqi sovereignty at "presidential" sites, limiting weapons inspection activities.

December: UNSCOM reports that Iraq is not complying with weapons inspections; Iraq claims that the United States is using

UNSCOM as a vehicle for spying on Iraq; the United States conducts an air and cruise missile campaign against Iraqi military targets (Operation Desert Fox); the Arab world and France, Russia, and China protest the bombings; Saddam Hussein remains defiant; UNSCOM inspections remain suspended; the U.S. Congress passes the Iraq Liberation Act, authorizing $97 million in military and other aid to Iraqi opposition groups.

1999
The United States and Britain pursue an aggressive bombing campaign against Iraq under the leadership of Clinton.

2000
April 13: The UN Security Council approves Resolution 1284, creating the Monitoring, Verification, and Inspection Commission (UNMOVIC) to replace UNSCOM and to oversee the destruction of Iraqi weapons; Iraq refuses to accept the new weapons inspection program.
August: UNMOVIC confirms that it has a new group of weapons inspectors trained for inspections in Iraq; Iraq continues to refuse to admit weapons inspectors.

2001
February 16 and 22: Under the administration of George W. Bush, U.S. aircraft attack air defense targets around Baghdad and in a northern no-fly zone after they were targeted by antiaircraft guns and Iraqi radar; the bombing is criticized by Arab nations and some European allies.
July: The UN is unable to agree on a loosening of economic sanctions, called "smart" sanctions, and the old sanctions program is extended; weapons inspections remain suspended.
September 11: The U.S. World Trade Center and the Pentagon are attacked by Arab terrorists. Later, reports surface of a meeting in Prague earlier in 2001 between suicide hijacker Mohammed Atta and an Iraqi intelligence agent, but these reports cannot be confirmed and no further evidence of Iraqi complicity in the September 11 attacks emerges.
October 7: The United States and Britain launch a war in Afghanistan to eliminate terrorists and overthrow the Taliban regime, which had supported al-Qaeda, the terrorist group responsible for the September 11 attacks.

2002

January 29: Bush announces in his State of the Union speech that Iraq is one of three countries forming an "axis of evil," threatening the world by supporting terrorists and developing weapons of mass destruction. Thereafter, Bush and administration officials repeatedly make comments indicating support for a regime change in Iraq, while European allies and Arab states indicate strong opposition to any attack on Iraq.

September 9: French president Jacques Chirac, in an interview, announces France's disagreement with the U.S. policy of preemptive attack on Iraq and urges the United States to work with the UN.

September 12: Bush addresses the UN, outlining Hussein's disregard for multiple UN resolutions and asking for UN help in neutralizing the threat that Iraq's weapons of mass destruction pose.

November 8: The UN Security Council unanimously adopts Resolution 1441, which provides Iraq "a final opportunity to comply with [UN] disarmament obligations," sets up "an enhanced [weapons] inspection regime," and warns Iraq that it will "face serious consequences" if it continues to violate UN-imposed obligations; inspectors return to Iraq in late November.

2003

January 9: Dr. Hans Blix, head of the new weapons inspection team, reports to the UN that the team has been given unfettered access to Iraq and that no weapons of mass destruction have been found. However, he also reports that Iraq has not provided a full and complete declaration of its weapons programs. Blix makes two more reports to the UN in February and March, similarly reporting no weapons of mass destruction and stating that Iraq is offering only limited cooperation.

February 5: U.S. secretary of state Colin Powell speaks at the UN and presents the U.S. case against Iraq, revealing numerous bits of U.S. intelligence information to show that Iraq is concealing its weapons of mass destruction from UN inspectors.

February 24: The United States, Britain, and Spain circulate a second UN resolution to authorize war against Iraq, stating that "Iraq has failed to take the final opportunity afforded to it [by] resolution 1441." The resolution is opposed by Germany, France, and Russia, which circulate a memo at the UN urging that war must be a last resort and that inspections must be continued. In March China joins the opposition group.

March 16: After a meeting with British prime minister Tony Blair and Spanish prime minister Jose Maria Anzar in the Azores, Bush indicates that a U.S. strike on Iraq is imminent.

March 17: Bush, in a speech to the nation, gives Hussein and his sons forty-eight hours to leave Iraq or face a U.S. military action. The following day, UN weapons inspectors leave Iraq.

March 18: Powell announces that the United States has assembled a "coalition of the willing" that includes some thirty nations supporting the military strike on Iraq.

March 19: The U.S. war begins in Iraq with a U.S. missile strike on Baghdad that is intended to kill Hussein. The strike is unsuccessful, and shortly thereafter air strikes begin pounding Iraq; air strikes are followed by a ground assault.

March 24: U.S.-led ground forces begin a march toward Baghdad but meet resistance from sandstorms and Saddam Hussein's troops.

April 9: U.S. troops take Baghdad, and jubilant Iraqis, with help from American marines, topple a huge statue of Saddam Hussein. The military thereafter secures various cities and towns in Iraq, searches for Saddam Hussein and other Baath Party officials, looks for weapons of mass destruction, and begins efforts to restore order to Iraq, where looting is prevalent.

April 15: Bush declares that the Saddam Hussein regime had ended.

April 28: More than two hundred delegates from inside and outside Iraq meet to discuss Iraq's future government.

May 2: Bush declares that major combat operations in Iraq have ended.

♦ FOR FURTHER RESEARCH

Books

Amatzia Baram, *Culture, History, and Ideology in the Formation of Ba'athist Iraq*. New York: Macmillan, 1991.

George Bush and Brent Scowcroft, *A World Transformed*. New York: Alfred Knopf, 1998.

Richard Butler, *The Greatest Threat*. New York: PublicAffairs, 2000.

Shahram Chubin and Charles Tripp, *Iran and Iraq at War*. Boulder, CO: Westview, 1988.

Anthony H. Cordesman and Ahmed Hashim, *Iraq: Sanctions and Beyond*. Boulder, CO: Westview, 1997.

Adel Darwish and Gregory Alexander, *Unholy Babylon: The Secret History of Saddam's War*. New York: St. Martin's, 1991.

Michael Eisenstadt, *Like a Phoenix from the Ashes? The Future of Iraqi Military Power*. Washington, DC: Washington Institute for Near East Policy, 1993.

Graham Fuller and Rend Francke, *The Arab Shi'a: The Forgotten Muslims*. New York: St. Martin's, 1999.

Efraim Karsh, *The Iran-Iraq War: Impact and Implications*. New York: St. Martin's, 1988.

Efraim Karsh and Inari Rautsi, *Saddam Hussein: A Political Biography*. New York: Macmillan, 1991.

Abbas Kelidar, *The Integration of Modern Iraq*. New York: St. Martin's, 1979.

Majid Khadduri, *War in the Gulf: The Iraq-Kuwait Conflict and Its Implications*. Oxford, UK: Oxford University Press, 1997.

Sandra Mackey, *The Reckoning: Iraq and the Legacy of Saddam Hussein*. New York: W.W. Norton, 2002.

Phebe Marr, *Iraq, Troubles and Tension: Persian Gulf Futures I*. Washington, DC: National Defense University, Institute for National Strategic Studies, 1997.

————, *The Modern History of Iraq.* Boulder, CO: Westview, 1985.

Susan Meisalis, *Kurdistan: In the Shadow of History.* London: Random House, 1997.

Yitzhak Nakash, *The Shi'is of Iraq.* Princeton, NJ: Princeton University Press, 1994.

Milan Rai, *War Plan Iraq.* New York: Verso, 2002.

Scott Ritter, *Endgame: Solving the Iraq Problem—Once and for All.* New York: Simon and Schuster, 1999.

George Roux, *Ancient Iraq.* Cleveland: World, 1965.

Geoff Simons, *Targeting Iraq: Sanctions and Bombing in U.S. Policy.* London: Saqi Books, 2002.

U.S. Library of Congress, *Iraq, a Country Study.* Ed. Helen Chapin Metz. Washington, DC, 1988.

Periodicals and Newspapers

Abdulkhaleq Abdulla, "Gulf War: The Socio-Political Background," *Arab Studies Quarterly*, Summer 1994.

Abbas Alnasrawi, "Iraq: Economic Sanctions and Consequences, 1990–2000," *Third World Quarterly*, April 2000.

William M. Arkin, "UNSCOM R.I.P.," *Bulletin of Atomic Scientists*, March/April 1999.

Associated Press, "Baghdad Says U.S. Is 'Lying' About Iraqi Weapons Program," *New York Times*, August 12, 2002.

Amatzia Baram, "Between Impediment and Advantage: Saddam's Iraq," *United States Institute of Peace*, June 1998.

Peter Beinart, "War Paths," *New Republic*, February 18, 2002.

Daniel Byman, "The Rollback Fantasy: Using the Iraqi Opposition to Oust Saddam Hussein Would Lead to a Replay of the Bay of Pigs," *Foreign Affairs*, January/February 1999.

Nancy Cooper, "After the War: Iraq's Designs; Hussein's Ambitions Are to Modernize His Country and Lay Claim to the Leadership of the Arab World," *Newsweek*, August 8, 1988.

Anthony H. Cordesman, "The Changing Military Balance in the Gulf," *Middle East Policy*, June 1998.

Adeed Dawisha, "'Identity' and Political Survival in Saddam's Iraq," *Middle East Journal*, Autumn 1999.

Charles A. Duelfer, "Why Iraq Will Never Give Up Its Worst Weapons," *Aviation Week and Space Technology*, March 11, 2002.

Gregg Easterbrook, "The Big One: The Real Danger Is Nuclear," *New Republic*, November 5, 2001.

Economist, "Know Thine Enemy—Weapons Proliferation: Where the World's Hidden and Not-So-Hidden Nuclear, Chemical, and Biological Weapons Are," February 2, 2002.

——, "Smart Exit: Sanctions on Iraq," July 7, 2001.

Foreign Affairs, "The Road to War," Winter 1991.

Michael M. Gunter, "The Iraqi Opposition and the Failure of U.S. Intelligence," *International Journal of Intelligence and Counterintelligence*, Summer 1999.

——, "The KDP-PUK Conflict in Northern Iraq," *Middle East Journal*, Spring 1996.

Denis Halliday, "Iraq and the UN's Weapon of Mass Destruction: Humanitarian Costs of Sanctions," *Current History*, February 1999.

Fred Halliday, "The Gulf War and Its Aftermath: First Reflections," *International Affairs*, April 1991.

Stephen Howe, "Backs to the Wall," *New Statesman and Society*, August 24, 1990.

Ed Kashi, "Struggle of the Kurds," *National Geographic*, August 1992.

Arthur Kent, "Girding for a Post-War Battle," *Maclean's*, April 14, 2003.

Andrew Lawler, "Destruction in Mesopotamia," *Science*, July 6, 2001.

Kamil Mahdi, "Rehabilitation Prospects for the Iraqi Economy," *International Spectator*, July/September 1998.

Phebe Marr, "Iraq's Uncertain Future," *Current History*, January 1991.

Joshua Micah Marshall, "Bomb Saddam?" *Washington Monthly*, June 2002.

Regis W. Matlak, "Inside Saddam's Grip," *National Security Studies Quarterly*, Spring 1999.

Robert McAdams, "Iraq's Cultural Heritage: Collateral Damage," *Science*, July 6, 2001.

David McDowall, "The Kurds: An Historical Perspective," *Asian Affairs*, October 1991.

Judith Miller, "Iraq Accused: A Case of Genocide," *New York Times Magazine*, January 3, 1993.

————, "Iraqi Tells of Renovations at Sites for Chemical and Nuclear Arms," *New York Times*, December 20, 2001.

James W. Moore, "Apres Saddam, Le Deluge? Speculating on Post-Saddam Iraq," *Middle East Policy*, February 1999.

Isabel O'Keefe, "The Silent Killer," *New Statesman and Society*, October 28, 1988.

Robert Olson, "The Kurdish Question Four Years On: The Policies of Turkey, Syria, Iran, and Iraq," *Middle East Policy*, Summer 1994.

George Perkovich, "Bush's Nuclear Revolution: A Regime Change in Nonproliferation," *Foreign Affairs*, March/April 2003.

Christopher Phillips, "Iraq Update: Still Unclear How Much Damage Was Inflicted on Archaeological and Cultural Sites in Iraq During the Allied Bombing Campaign," *Art-in-America*, May 1991.

Daniel Pipes and Laurie Mylroie, "Back Iraq: It's Time for a U.S. 'Tilt'," *New Republic*, April 27, 1987.

Alan Pogue, "Collateral Damage: Iraq Under the Sanctions," *U.S. Catholic*, August 2001.

Kenneth M. Pollack, "Iraq and the United States: Ready for War," *Foreign Affairs*, March/April 2002.

William Safire, "Saddam's Offensive," *New York Times*, April 8, 2002.

Brent Scowcroft, "Scowcroft on Iraq," *Business Week*, April 8, 2002.

Max Singer, "The Chalabi Factor," *National Review*, April 14, 2003.

Jed C. Snyder, "The Road to Osiraq: Baghdad's Quest for the Bomb," *Middle East Journal*, Autumn 1983.

Chuck Sudetic, "The Betrayal of Basra," *Mother Jones*, November/ December 2001.

Time, "Inside Saddam's World," May 13, 2002.

U.S. Congress, "Disarming Iraq: The Status of Weapons Inspections," September 15, 1998.

Al J. Venter, "How Saddam Almost Built His Bomb," *Middle East Policy*, February 1999.

Susan Wright, "The Hijacking of UNSCOM," *Bulletin of the Atomic Scientists*, May/June 1999.

Paul Zimansky and Elizabeth C. Stone, "Mesopotamia in the Aftermath of the Gulf War," *Archaeology*, May/June 1992.

Stephen Zunes, "Confrontation with Iraq: A Bankrupt U.S. Policy," *Middle East Policy*, June 1998.

Websites

Iraq Action Coalition, http://leb.net. An online media and resource center for groups and activists who are working to end the economic sanctions against the people of Iraq.

The Iraq Foundation, www.iraqfoundation.org. A nonprofit, nongovernmental organization working for democracy and human rights in Iraq.

Iraq Watch, www.iraqwatch.org. A website devoted to monitoring Iraq's progress in building weapons of mass destruction.

The Nonviolence Web, Iraq Crisis Anti-War Homepage, www.nonviolence.org. This website is home to dozens of major U.S. peace groups, all of whom have been organizing against another war in the Persian Gulf.

United Nations, Office of the Iraq Programme Oil-for-Food, www.un.org. A UN website providing information about the oil-for-food program established by Security Council Resolution 986 in 1995.

U.S. Central Intelligence Agency (CIA), www.cia.gov. A government website providing geographical, political, economic, and other information on the country of Iraq.

U.S. Department of State, International Information Programs, http://usinfo.state.gov. A government website providing information about current political issues and human rights involving Iraq.

🔥 INDEX

Abbas, Abu, 76
Ahmed, Rafeeudin, 92–93
Airborne Warning and Control Systems
  (AWACS), 42
Albu Nasir tribe, 28
al-Da'wa al-Islamiyya. See Islamic Call
Alexander (Iraqi ruler), 23
Algeria, 71
Algiers Agreement (1975), 25
Andianna Café, 31
Anfal campaign, 44–51
Aref, Abd al-Salaam, 31
Arif government, 39
arms sales. *See* military aid
assassinations, 32
Assyria, 23

Baath Party, 15, 27
  assassinations and, 33
  CIA-assisted coup by, 31
  Hussein's early years in, 29
  Hussein's rise to power in, 31–32
Babylon, 23
Bacon, Kenneth, 92
Baghdad Pact (1958), 38
Baker, James, 53
Bakhtiar, Shahpour, 36–37
Bakr, Ahmad Hasan al, 3, 15–16, 28, 31,
  33, 36
Bani-Sadr, Hassan, 37
Barzani, Mustafa, 101
Batatu, Hanna, 29
Begin, Menachem, 40
al-Bejat clan, 28
Blair, Tony
  criticism of, 107
  on Iraq's oil resources, 82
  on weapons of mass destruction, 69, 70
  see also Great Britain
Blix, Hans, 77
Brazil, 39, 40
Brown, Mark Malloch, 91–92
Bush, George H.W., 52
Bush, George W., 58
  criticism of, 12
  declaring war on Iraq and, 11, 59–62
  distrust and criticism of, 110–11

on Iraq's oil resources, 82
reasons for Iraq War by, 11–12
on threat of Iraq, 59
on threat of terrorism, 61–62
on weapons of mass destruction, 12–13

Carroll, Philip, 84
Carter, Jimmy, 41
Central Intelligence Agency (CIA), 31,
  40–41
Chalabi, Ahmad, 65, 78
chemical attacks, 45, 47, 49–50
Cheney, Dick, 12
Chevron Texaco, 82
China, 13, 84
Chirac, Jacques, 38
Cirincione, Joseph, 77, 91, 109
Cockburn, Andrew, 26
Cockburn, Patrick, 26
Corn, David, 67
coup attempts
  overthrowing Qassim and, 31
  pro-Shah of Iran and, 36–37
Critchfield, James, 31
Cyrus (Iraqi ruler), 23

Darius (Iraqi ruler), 23
Dawa party, 36, 100
Da-wa Islamiyah. See Islamic Call
democracy
  promise of, in postwar Iraq, 97–98
  U.S. dream for Iraqi, 77–78
  was not a goal in Iraq War, 70–71
Department of Homeland Security, 62
d' Estaing, Giscard, 38
Dulles, Allen, 27

Eagleton, William, 41–42
Eastern Europe, 66
economic sanctions against Iraq, 17,
  18–19, 53
Economist (magazine), 81
Egypt, 30–31
Eitan, Rafael, 40
ethnic divisions
  Great Britain's exclusion of Shiites
    from power and, 98–99